CHASING
PERFECTION

CHASING PERFECTION

SHATTER THE ILLUSION

MINIMIZE SELF-DOUBT & MAXIMIZE SUCCESS

Sue Hawkes

with Alexandra Stieglbauer

Advantage®

Published by Advantage, Charleston, South Carolina.
Member of Advantage Media Group.

ADVANTAGE is a registered trademark, and the Advantage colophon is a trademark of Advantage Media Group, Inc.

Printed in the United States of America.

10 9 8 7 6 5 4 3 2 1

ISBN: 978-1-59932-846-1
LCCN: 2017954058

Cover design by Melanie Cloth.
Layout design by Megan Elger.

This publication is designed to provide accurate and authoritative information in regard to the subject matter covered. It is sold with the understanding that the publisher is not engaged in rendering legal, accounting, or other professional services. If legal advice or other expert assistance is required, the services of a competent professional person should be sought.

Advantage Media Group is proud to be a part of the Tree Neutral® program. Tree Neutral offsets the number of trees consumed in the production and printing of this book by taking proactive steps such as planting trees in direct proportion to the number of trees used to print books. To learn more about Tree Neutral, please visit **www.treeneutral.com.**

TreeNeutral

Advantage Media Group is a publisher of business, self-improvement, and professional development books. We help entrepreneurs, business leaders, and professionals share their Stories, Passion, and Knowledge to help others Learn & Grow. Do you have a manuscript or book idea that you would like us to consider for publishing? Please visit advantagefamily.com or call **1.866.775.1696.**

This book is dedicated to my amazing husband and partner in life, Kevin, who shows up every day as the finest person I've ever known. I'm grateful to love you and be loved by you. Our tether is tangible.

To our terrific children, Alexandra, Quinton, and Summer; your love and our incredible adventures fuel me as we continue to define our best version of what it means to be a chosen family. I'm better because of all of you, and together we are unstoppable!

Portions of this book were first published in Sue Hawkes's column "Inspiring Women" and are printed here with permission of *Minnesota Business* magazine.

TABLE OF CONTENTS

ACKNOWLEDGMENTS . . . . **xi**

INTRODUCTION **1**

CHAPTER ONE **5**

UNMASKING YOUR SUPERHERO

This chapter explores the self-doubt many leaders experience, also known as imposter syndrome. Vulnerability is explored in this chapter, along with practices focusing on leading with vulnerability and asking for help.

CHAPTER TWO **17**

BALANCE IS BULLSHIT

This chapter explores the myth of balance and the many roles leaders are pulled into: business owner, confidant, mentor, leader, manager, spouse, teammate, friend—the list goes on. It includes practices for managing these roles and assessing when you are misaligned with your own values. We explore the cost of saying yes, how to say no effectively, and how to delegate, without guilt, things that aren't the highest and best use of your time.

CHAPTER THREE **31**

PUT ON YOUR OXYGEN MASK FIRST

This chapter discusses self-care and provides healthy practices to change your thinking and overcome the habit of putting yourself last. Do you take care of everyone else around you at your own expense? It's time to stop. As a leader, you can better serve others when you first take care of yourself. We highlight leaders who have overcome challenging issues such as addiction and anxiety as they pursue the path to a healthier self.

CHAPTER FOUR **43**

CONQUERING CATASTROPHE

This chapter explores when the events of your business and life are occurring at such a fast pace and on such a life-altering scale that nothing would have prepared you for them. As a leader, how do you dig deep to find the energy, commitment, and drive to continue moving forward amidst overwhelming circumstances?

CHAPTER FIVE **61**

INTUITION IS YOUR SUPERPOWER

This chapter explores using your intuition as a strategic influence in your business and life. As a leader, how do you lead with, and follow, your intuition—especially amidst "logical" counterarguments? The emphasis is on quieting your limiting self-talk and learning to trust yourself.

CHAPTER SIX **77**

GAME CHANGERS AND TRAILBLAZERS

This chapter highlights leaders who changed the business world by paving the way for others. How do we learn from these game changers and lead without apologizing? How do we forge new trails while eliminating the barriers that don't serve us and bring others along for the ride?

CHAPTER SEVEN **89**

BACKWARD AND IN HEELS

This chapter explores the excellence and mastery it takes to become an exceptional business leader. Women leaders must be willing to go the extra mile, deliver what's possible, and work to always improve, regardless of limits or what may seem reasonable to others.

CHAPTER EIGHT **101**

POURING GAS ON THE FIRE

This chapter explores how to identify what triggers your optimal performance. For many leaders, the ultimate driver is having a positive impact on the world. The emphasis is on discovering your purpose and designing practices to align them with your business goals.

CHAPTER NINE **113**

UNLEARNING TO LEARN

This chapter explores the connection between lifelong learning and success. Unlearning those habits that hinder you allows you to be coachable, humble, and creative. We explain how success can be a learning disability and identify the practices to unleash your maximum potential.

CHAPTER TEN **127**

ENTITLED TO ENLIGHTENED

This chapter explores how to simplify working effectively between generations. Belief in generational stereotypes limits your ability to harness the best from everyone at the table. Learn how to unlock potential from all generations by engaging everyone around shared values. The emphasis is on gracefully communicating through the tough stuff.

CONCLUSION. **143**

LEADERS IN THIS BOOK **145**

WAYS TO REACH US **147**

REFERENCES. **149**

ACKNOWLEDGMENTS

I want to acknowledge all the incredible leaders who've inspired and taught me. This book is the culmination of all I've learned from you, and it wouldn't have been possible without the support and contribution of the following list of people. I will never be able to thank you enough for your impact on me, my life, my work, and my family.

To name them all would require too many pages, so I'll include the VIPs on my list.

Joyce and Bill Hawkes Sr., my mom and dad. Your love and strong values have guided me to do the right thing and always be a contributor in life. You were the best parents I could've asked for; I miss you both dearly and hope this book would have made you proud.

rubye Erickson, my Edina mom. You taught me how to be a professional in dress and demeanor. You define excellence and demonstrate it always, requiring the best of yourself and those around you. I'd be lost in the fashion world without you. My life is richer because of our adventures together.

Cheryl Regan, my teammate and friend. You are the epitome of what it means to be a servant leader. Always ready with "How can I help?" and ready to lend a hand no matter what. Three companies, many laughs, tears, and so many great stories created together. Nothing gets done without you; thank you for who you are and all you do.

Alexandra Stieglbauer, my daughter with no stretch marks. Thank you for being a terrific leader, learner, and teammate. Working together every day and on this book has been a dream come true. You are a force. I'm proud of you and grateful to be your mom. You care deeply and work hard daily to serve in excellence. You are a loving, talented, poised, and beautiful woman inside and out. This world is ready for your voice. Your contribution to this book (especially chapter 10) is only the beginning! Thank you for the sweat, extra hours, and detail you bring every day. I am excited for you and us; we did it!

Quinton Coffman (Q), my son. Thank you for being a loving, caring, creative, generous man in this world. You are the reason I persevered. It wasn't always easy for us, but we made it, and you are incredible. You taught me about learning, letting go, and loving fiercely. Every day, I'm proud of you and grateful to be your mom.

Summer Stieglbauer, my daughter with no stretch marks. Thank you for accepting us, being willing to do fun things together, and loving good food and great travel. You are a superstar, smart, honest, hardworking, and beautiful. I am proud of you and all you do. I'm grateful to be your mom.

Vern and Linda Stieglbauer, my incredible in-laws. Thanks for loving us into your family. You are the epitome of care. You set the bar for being fantastic parents; you are truly good people creating an inclusive, loving family. I aspire to follow in your footsteps.

Bill Jr., Gary, and Dan Hawkes, my big brothers. I am grateful for your love and care. You each have taught me so much, whether I wanted to learn or not! You are the best brothers I could ask for. I miss Bill; he died too soon.

Rhoda Olsen, my mentor and friend. Thank you for meeting with me and teaching me in all you say and do. You are the consummate leader and I am grateful you make time for me. I learn from your actions and words; you are walking integrity.

Gino Wickman, humble, passionate, and intense teacher and leader. Thank you for being the genius behind the work, which allows me (and *so* many others) to live the incredible lives we do. Your impact is making a great big dent in this universe and I'm happy to be a small part of that movement. Without you, I wouldn't have written this book.

Bettie Spruill, former business partner. Thank you for the spiritual depth and learning you've provided me. I would not be who I am, living the life I am, without you.

Beth Leonard and Giannina Hall, heroes and advisors on Earth. Without you and your unbelievable generosity at a time when life held little hope, I may have walked a very different path. You showed up at my greatest time of need and gave without asking for a thing, providing a work-home and a home. Thank you for treating a lifeline as an everyday act. What seemed very minor to you changed my life. Your grace is an example I work to pay forward.

To the leaders featured in this book who are called out on their own page. You are the inspiration for me to write this book. Thank you for carving the path, standing out, and speaking up. You are heroes in our world, living, breathing examples of leaders who won't settle and call others up to playing a bigger game. Thank you for doing the hard work so many can lead in their way; we need you.

Dr. Marsha Firestone, founder of the Women Presidents' Organization (WPO). Thank you for being a trailblazer for women in business. Because of you, I have sisters and a community to learn with, guiding me in business and life.

Myrna Marofsky, all members of WPO MN, Platinum 6, and all the WPO Chapter Chairs. Thank you for teaching me to learn, love, and lead in business. I love our sisterhood.

The Honey Badgers and all EOS Implementers™, thank you for being a stellar tribe of people who care deeply, do the right thing, help others to live their ideal lives, and challenge me to be better every day.

Lisa Oppegard, Carla Anderson, Carla Bainbridge, Colleen Kleve, Anita Janssen, and my friends. The happy hours, support, love, listening, laughs, and tears together got me here. You are my bedrock when the stuff hits the fan. Thanks for always reminding me of who I am and what's possible during tough times and being ready to celebrate the good times. Our happy days together outweigh any pitfalls. I don't know where I'd be without you—thanks for making memories with me.

Dawn Brommer, Anita Janssen, Jennifer Laible, Max Lipset, and Alexandra and Kevin Stieglbauer for reviewing and editing the book. Thanks for taking the time to make it better. You took coal and made it a diamond. Ali and Kev, you are the best team I could ask for at home and work—thanks for the hours and detail. I love you both.

To my clients, graduates, and participants over the past twenty-five-plus years, thank you for trusting me with your lives and businesses. You give me the opportunity to do work I love. I am humbled and inspired by your dedication and hard work, passion to win, commitment to do the right thing, willingness to challenge what you know, care for your people, ability to solve problems, and drive to make our world better. You make every day worthwhile.

STOP!!!!

READ THIS FIRST.

Before you begin doing what you've always done with every book before this, let me help you get the most from your reading.

1. This book is not intended to be read cover to cover. You're free to read any and all chapters that are most relevant to you right now and ignore the rest. You can pick it up at any time when it makes sense. That's what you'll do anyway.

2. This book is written for entrepreneurs, business owners, leaders, and those aspiring to be one of those three things. Is there anyone else?

3. A few chapters are written specifically for women in one of the categories mentioned in number two. If you're a realized man, with strong emotional intelligence, you'll get it and make the connections. If you're neither a woman leader nor a realized man, you can ignore these chapters, as you've likely ignored these perspectives.

4. This book has several stories from my life in it. Some are personal, which are more uncomfortable for me to share. Some are professional and meant to represent the thousands of people I've worked with. You see, I work in a world of confidentiality and only the people named agreed to share their stories. So I offer myself as an example to demonstrate the points I'm making. Please draw your own conclusions, knowing I'm representing a lot of experience with each story. You can use them or lose them at will. I do.

5. I'm writing this with the intention of inspiring you, the reader, to *stop* chasing perfection and shatter that illusion. When you do the work I've outlined in this book (and at www.ChasingPerfection.net), and you are consistently practicing what I've offered, you will be more confident and able to maximize success. For those who join this movement to shatter the illusion, mastery entails becoming unf♥<kwithable in the process. And that's the point.

6. What's unf♥<kwithability you ask? You'll find out when you complete each chapter, as we've included links with bonus information, practices, and resources for you to explore. The rest of you will skip to the end of the book and read the conclusion, as you always do, and that's the shortcut you're looking for. I can't believe you've read all of these instructions; most leaders wouldn't!

INTRODUCTION

I built my first business in fifth grade and dragged my friend Amy into it. We were opposites, which seems to be the great start for most business partnerships. Amy was the more conservative, thoughtful, risk-averse partner; I was the risk-taking, big-thinking, and door-opening partner. We knew how to make macramé plant hangers. The two of us could make two to four plant hangers every night and even more if we had the weekend to work. My dad mimeographed our business cards on the powder-blue card stock I had purchased at Woolworths. (We didn't have copiers yet—my God, I feel old writing this!) We cut those cards with the kitchen scissors. Our company name was a blend of our two last names and we included our parents' rotary-dial, home phone numbers. The cost of our materials was about ten cents a pound, plus our time. Our mark-up was about 900 percent. We went door-to-door and sold the plant hangers—a lot of them, enough that I could lose about $200 from my bike's pannier (it seemed secure!), after which Amy took over as the banker. It was a good choice. We made about $500 after our loss, which we used to buy Christmas presents for our families. That was it; game over. We accomplished what we had intended to and the company was finished. Little did I know that experience would set the stage for my future as an entrepreneur.

At the age of eleven, I learned you could make as much money as you could work for, and I was willing to work hard for it. Through college, I went to school full-time, worked full-time, and still found time to paint murals freelance. I was always motivated to make money and do things I'd never done before. Most of my jobs when I was growing up were leadership positions, from managing a restaurant to running a company by the time I was twenty-six. God knows, as a liberal arts major, I had no idea what I was doing, and to no surprise, that company went out of business a few years later. I learned more at that little company, where I cut my teeth in the training business and failed forward, than anywhere else. I was presenting to audiences of twenty to a hundred people, consisting of students, CEOs, and everyone in between. First, I was leading guest events and then doing small pieces of our training, and by the time I was twenty-seven, I was leading ninety-day leadership programs that included a significant community service component. It was intense, unreasonable, and extraordinarily transformational work—and I loved it.

That was the springboard for my future. I found my life's work in leading workshops, keynotes, and seminars in my twenties. My work included general public training sessions as well as working with CEOs of multimillion-dollar businesses through the Women Presidents' Organization (WPO), which you'll see mentioned throughout this book. That's one way I continue to learn about business: from the incredible women who support and challenge one another in the WPO. Balancing running my own company, being a chapter chair for WPO, and leading workshops had been my fuel for years. As you'll read, I had two companies throughout my thirties and forties. I founded a global coaching certification program, and I continue to lead my company YESS!®. I've worked with leaders and their teams for the bulk of my career. My keynotes and workshops focus on topics including: effective communication, coaching, leadership development, emotional intelligence, and team performance. I have all kinds of certifications and acronyms, as I enjoy learning so much; it seems I'm either leading a program or attending one most of the time.

In 2013, I became certified in the Entrepreneurial Operating System® (EOS®). It was one of the best things I've done because it married my passion for working with entrepreneurial leadership teams, communication, team health, and making a difference. I love my mix of work and the people I serve.

So why write this book now? Good question. As I sit editing it for the gazillionth time, I'm wondering the same thing! In all seriousness, I have several reasons and you'll recognize a theme. First, like most leaders, I want to accomplish something on a grander scale. My team and I will continue to work with leadership teams directly, yet I can also dramatically increase the number of people I impact by writing this book. Second, my intent is for the book to be so useful it creates more opportunities to reach wider audiences with keynotes and workshops. Third, my kids: I want them to understand they can avoid the mistakes I've made if they get a head-start on these practices and apply themselves to their passions. They may not be able to hear it from me, yet perhaps if it's in writing, they will be three of the people most favorably impacted. Frankly, that's what I'm hoping for every reader. Fourth, I've been asked by many people over the years to write a book so they can share me, in a sense. If that will impact more people, I'm willing. So, in short, it's about the number of humans positively impacted by me.

Why this format? Because I've heard the same challenges echoed from too many hardworking, generous, sincerely great leaders, and I'm hoping this will mitigate some of the pain and help leaders—like you—thrive. Most of you are rule breakers by nature, so reading cover to cover is unlikely anyway. Many of you never finish a book. You're great starters, however, so suggesting you find the most compelling chapter(s) and begin there will make sense for most of you. It's what you'd do anyway. Besides, the format allowed me to thematically present the struggles I hear most often behind closed doors. I hope you won't just read this book; it's really important you *do* something about whatever you read if it pertains to you. This is not a passive read; it's an active read. Throughout this book there are practices and suggestions for what to do to help shatter any illusion you may have.

I've wasted too much time, energy, and money chasing perfection and I'm done with it. I want to shatter the illusion and bring everyone I can with me. Our tribe of learners will move forward together, helping others to lead with grace, shatter the illusions we're full of, and end our needless suffering in pursuit of perfection. It will require two things: vulnerability and the support of the people around you. It can be done, and it takes practice. Once you master what's between these pages, you'll be unf♥<kwithable. So start reading, find out what that means, and get on your way!

CHAPTER ONE

UNMASKING YOUR SUPERHERO

It's not who you are that holds you back;
it's who you think you're not.

—Denis Waitley, motivational speaker and success expert

The best advice I've ever received is "No one
else knows what they're doing either."

—Ricky Gervais, award-winning comedian and television writer

Most of the leaders I know, myself included, project a competent, confident exterior to the world. Yet beneath that calm public exterior lurks the fear of being found out as a fraud: *What if they discover I'm not who I'm pretending to be?* Or *I don't really know what I'm doing. I'm just making it up as I go along.* Interestingly, the more successful the leader is, the louder and more persistent those voices can become. How many of us go through our lives and careers feeling like we're faking it (and might get caught)? The better questions are: when does it begin and what can you do about it?

In 1978 the term *imposter syndrome* was coined by clinical psychologists Pauline R. Clance and Suzanne A. Imes, describing high-achieving individuals who are marked by an inability to internalize their accomplishments and a persistent fear of being exposed as a fraud. Despite external evidence of their competence, those exhibiting the syndrome remain convinced they are frauds and do not deserve the success they've achieved. Research shows 70 to 80 percent of leaders experience imposter syndrome. In other words, if you haven't experienced self-doubt in this way, you're likely the imposter.

When we think there's no one who can possibly relate to all we're challenged with, what can we do? We can find other leaders who are facing similar challenges and with whom we feel comfortable enough to talk about it.

AGES AND STAGES

It starts early. When we are in our twenties, life is about proving ourselves and figuring out who we're going to be. In my twenties I wanted everybody to think I knew more than I did. I was out to conquer the world before breakfast; my parents told me I could do anything, and I believed them. When I got out into the world, the crashing reality hit: "Wow, there are a lot of really competent people out there. I'm not so special. I've got to work harder." That realization drove me to be overly competitive and it threw life out of balance. Fortunately, I discovered volunteering: When I started to put my energy into serving others and began to focus outward, I realized it wasn't all about me, and things started to become a lot easier. I was able to measure myself more honestly: to look at other people in my sphere and recognize just how much I had to learn. It was a lot (and seems to become more every day)—and that's okay.

MAXIMIZE SUCCESS

Beth Bronfman

Now managing partner of View, The Agency, Beth began her career at Lane Bryant, eventually moving on to Macy's where she became VP of advertising and then left to start her own firm. Despite a career path that might appear to an onlooker as a line going straight up, she admits, "When I was younger, I did have more doubts. Most people do. I think the older you get, the more you realize that things really do work out. It may not be the way you expect it to be, but I think it's the way it's supposed to be. That's a lesson you learn with age. You have to be resilient and flexible. You have to bounce back. In the beginning, when I started my business, I would get nervous about everything. "Am I going to get this deal? Is it going to work out right?" It doesn't bother me anymore, because I know that it will work out. That's part of the journey of life, right? And if you have a good marriage and love for your family, it makes everything so much better."

Her advice to young people? "Be resilient. People like to critique things because it makes them feel important. But you've got to just listen, take a little grain from it, and move on. You can't get yourself in knots and say, 'Oh my God, they hated it. I can't go on.' Forget it; you've got to move on. People who can't let things go get moody and wallow in the fact that someone hated their work, but you can't live your life like that. I wouldn't have a business in advertising if we didn't keep moving on and learning and evolving."

When asked what she attributes her success to, she answers with a question: "What's success? You always have to strive. It keeps you on your toes. I cannot rest on my laurels, because I know I'm only as good as my next campaign. You can't talk about all these great things you did in the past. You've got to do it now." For Beth, success is a journey, not a destination—and she treats every assignment with the same level of commitment she brought to her first job: "It doesn't matter if it's the smallest job or the biggest job. You have to give it the same billion percent effort. Every day is a new day and a new opportunity."

TAKING ON COMMITMENTS

In our thirties, life gets more complex as we take on new roles and responsibilities. Maybe we get married, have children, or buy a home. Suddenly, we've got greater accountability and more bills to pay. We can start to feel trapped in our career or by our other choices. Chucking it all and taking off for Europe is no longer an easy option; we're buying a couch or replacing the water heater, not going on spring break. We're learning to juggle our responsibilities. What you put on Facebook draws attention to all the cool things you're doing, but the reality is you have to decide whether you'll travel 40 percent of the time for your career or if you want to have a family, because those two don't always go together—and your spouse is wrestling with the same choices. So you bolster up your game face, don the mask of success, and start juggling it all.

When my mom was growing up, the career choices for women were nurse, schoolteacher, or secretary. The door cracked open for my generation, offering us many more options (in a business world designed by men for men). Yet somehow, we never discarded the idea that we also had to be stellar homemakers and parents in the same way our stay-at-home moms were. We were caught up in Martha Stewart perfectionism: our homes, our kids, and our careers all had to be perfect—*and* nobody should see us sweat while we were figuring it out.

The lack of internal confidence is real—and persistent. Somehow, no achievement is ever quite significant enough to reassure us we've arrived. The bar is always rising. For many business owners, the first landmark for growing a business is to reach a million dollars in revenue; it's the first big benchmark of "I did it!" Time and again I see leaders raising their goals without pausing to savor their success. Suddenly, the benchmark becomes $10 million because $1 million "just isn't that much." I've heard people with multimillion-dollar businesses say, "I've got a baby business" in comparison to other business owners. Somehow, they still see themselves as just barely qualified to be in the room with other leaders of larger businesses! And that nagging voice in their heads just gets louder—the one saying, "I'm a fake" or "I don't belong" or "How long can I go on fooling people?" or "What if they find out?"

The more successful we become, the less we allow ourselves to talk about the challenges we face, because that would crack the façade of how we appear to the world. So we quiet ourselves to protect the façade and become very lonely behind our mask of success.

PRACTICES FOR SUCCESS

Learn to Ask for Help and Be Willing to Receive It

I see leaders building trust and being honest about their issues within the business roundtable groups I facilitate and speak at when one person is willing to say, "It's a mess right now. Please don't pin me with this permanently. I need your support." Most leaders are phenomenally competent at so many things—I can't think of many leaders who aren't—yet admitting they're struggling is tough because they don't want to be judged or pop the perceived bubble of perfection. Among trusted peers, they feel safer and less exposed—and it's a tremendous relief for them to hear the person next to them say, "I've been there too." Once people open the door by admitting they're overwhelmed and need help, it creates permission for everyone to be vulnerable and tell the truth as well. It's hard to be the one to go first. Learning to express vulnerability, ask for help, and receive it gracefully are key skills for any leader's success.

HOW DOES OUR LACK OF SELF-CONFIDENCE HINDER US?

One of the most revealing differences between men and women is how they present themselves as job candidates, which exposes a chasm of self-confidence. When men are interviewing for a job, they're comfortable talking about how they can do whatever is required, even if they've never done it. If women are interviewing for the same job, they'll typically project much less self-assurance: "I haven't done it yet, but here's what I have done and I believe that indicates I can handle this as well." Women rely on what they've done, whereas men focus on how their experience is the *reason* they will be able to do something in the future. All things being equal, who do you think an employer is more likely to feel confident hiring in this scenario? Men will read a job description and if they meet at least half of the requirements, typically, they'll apply. Women will only apply if they meet a majority of the requirements. In cases like these, women would benefit from a bit of overconfidence and trusting a "fake it 'till you make it" mentality will pay off. Communicating from an honest place, while focusing on what your experience makes possible, will open more doors every time.

And now I'm going to sound like a hypocrite. Faking it—putting a game face on when you're not feeling confident—is another way we wear a mask. And there comes a point at which it's no longer an option—and I hit that point.

I am a chapter chair for the Women Presidents' Organization (WPO), and twelve of us decided to form a roundtable for ourselves. One evening, I was talking with one of the members before our conference call, and I remember saying to her, "Things are really hard right now." That was an understatement: My mother had been diagnosed with Alzheimer's, so I was cooking for my parents and taking care of Mom on weekends. I was providing for my family because my husband wasn't earning any income and had withdrawn into himself. He'd been in charge of paying the household accounts. However, it wasn't until I came across a certified envelope with my name on it, containing a foreclosure notice dated several months previously, buried in a stack of mail, that I learned he hadn't been making the house payments. That was the moment I finally decided to divorce him. Add that to the overfull life I was already living. I had to sell my house against a deadline and work with the bank to repair our relationship and our finances. Thankfully, I was able to sell in time, but it left me with only three weeks (which included some travel for work) to pack and move out, all while caring for my son and parents and running two businesses.

As I confessed this to my friend, the floodgates opened. I cried and admitted, "I've never felt like more of a failure." I didn't want to unload on everyone about my personal problems and I didn't know if I'd clearly communicate all that was happening.

"This is why we have this group," my friend said. "This is where you're going to be vulnerable. You're one of those people nobody assumes is challenged with anything."

That hit me like a two-by-four; "What? That can't be true." One insightful conversation made it possible for me to be on the conference call and put it *all* out there. I removed my mask and cape, sharing everything with them and letting them see my unmasked self, flaws and all.

I would never have had the courage to be that vulnerable if my WPO colleague had not challenged and encouraged me. As so many leaders are, I too was blind to my pride in masking my over-competent façade. I also thought it was selfish to open up—I didn't want to take up time that someone else in the group might need more than I did. Too often we stop ourselves from being vulnerable when we need to be. The more successful we are, the more we conceal, because now we have a public image to preserve—and if the world knows we're not perfect, we're concerned it could become a permanent black mark.

By the end of that conference call I felt a lot better, but I also worried that I'd blown my credibility. I remember thinking, *I feel like a fraud. I coach people about how to run effective businesses and how to live successful, fulfilling lives—yet my life is the antithesis of that.* In the coming days, I was relieved when the other group members reached out to me to offer support and share their own vulnerabilities with me. My self-disclosure proved to be a doorway to intimacy and depth in our relationships, which, in turn, made us stronger and more connected.

The greatest outcome? I'm more authentic and accessible as a result of that difficult period in my life. I make no bones about how removing my mask, sharing it all, and being vulnerable was the only way to move forward. I've made a lot of mistakes, and the sum of those now gives people permission to be vulnerable with me in return.

MAXIMIZE SUCCESS

Nancy Lyons

Nancy Lyons mixes well with people, has a wicked sense of humor, and is an easy person to like. From pursuing theater in college, doing stand-up comedy, and being on the national speaker's circuit, the charismatic CEO of Clockwork is the last person you'd imagine would suffer from a lack of self-confidence—but she admits, "Most people think I'm supremely confident but I don't always feel that way. I think confidence is something we talk a lot about in professional spaces and we either assume everyone has it or say they should get it. We don't talk about what it feels like or how normal it is to question confidence or to lack confidence. We also don't talk about how it feels in a service business to come to a table maybe second-guessing ourselves

> and how that could come across to the client. When that happens, how do we recover quickly and gain trust? We put ourselves through a lot. We humans are really hard on ourselves. But I've found that confidence comes more naturally when you really work hard to know your stuff and you commit to always telling the truth."

I was forty years old when I had to sell my home to avoid foreclosure. As I stood in my driveway with my home emptied and all my belongings packed, it was one of the most sobering moments of my life. My mind was running a continual loop which said, "I have been working my entire life and *everything* I own fits into a pod; one single pod." I was so busy packing and worrying about my son and my mom and my work and trying to get out on time so the house could sell and not go into foreclosure. What I hadn't given one shred of thought to was where in the world we were going to live next.

And that's when I took vulnerability to the next level. I began a group exercise in a coaching certification program I was leading by admitting, "I have no idea where I'm going to live. All my belongings are packed and in a pod. I would really appreciate if anybody has any great ideas for housing for my son, dogs, and me on short notice."

One of the people in that program was Giannina Hall, a woman I had previously coached. Giannina approached me during the break and said, "I have a furnished townhome where you can live. I would feel honored if you'd stay there in return for all you've done for me." A member of my staff also offered his basement to me. In a matter of minutes (and a huge swallow of pride), there were two offers, with no questions asked.

I broke down in tears. It was the most phenomenal example of how everything you need is available to you; you just have to ask for it. I didn't know how to say yes to her offer; I didn't know how I could pay her; I didn't even know if I had clean clothes for the next day. Everything was in boxes and bags. My options were slim and I had no time.

So, in this case, I couldn't say no. We ended up living in Gianinna's home for about five and a half months. She never charged me rent; she even paid the utilities. It was one of the most generous, unconditional gifts I've ever received, and it was incredibly humbling because I felt dependent upon someone beyond my family. At the same time, it completely changed my life.

PRACTICES FOR SUCCESS

The Doubler Exercise

The Doubler Exercise, created by Shawn Achor, is a daily practice meant to increase joy and gratitude, which in turn leads to better productivity and satisfaction in one's overall life. Every evening, write down the most meaningful experience you had that day. Then write down three details. Including the three details will cause you to reflect back on the moment and therefore achieve double the positive energy and benefits from the experience. You will also create a record of what is most meaningful to you and begin to notice a trend you can then intentionally act upon. Taking time to notice and reflect on a meaningful experience each day will train your mind to look for the positive in all things.

I'm the speaker onstage saying, "Keep your word; be accountable." I had done exactly that, yet it wasn't enough to avoid disaster in my personal life. I reached that point and realized there were choices to make and different ways to look at my situation. Recognizing that my previous choices had contributed to my current situation felt like the ultimate acceptance of accountability. I didn't have a clear perspective until I journaled, meditated, moved on, and *asked for and received* a ton of help—because I never could have accomplished all I did in that three-week period, or over the summer, without all the people around me who told me they could help me out and were happy to do so. I realized how much support was there for me once I stopped being too proud to ask for it. Pride limits us when it stops us from connecting with others. Are we afraid to look weak? Afraid to be indebted?

My life turned around, and I have a lot of people to thank for it. Amazingly, *not one of them expected a thing back*—and that was another tremendous lesson for me. I have prided myself on being a giver only to realize it's terribly selfish to refuse to accept someone else's help. When you won't accept help graciously, you're actually denying others the good feelings they would otherwise enjoy. My life was built around being the one doing the giving—and I didn't understand how selfish that was until I learned to receive the help offered. Giving makes us all feel good. By declining to receive, we're actually taking from others.

I learned many things from that difficult, humbling period in my life. The biggest lesson was that you'll never know how much others care about you until you take off your mask and let yourself be seen as you are, vulnerabilities, failings, and all—and perhaps having the courage to take off your mask is what makes you a superhero after all.

For bonus information, practices, and resources:
www.ChasingPerfection.net/book/chapter-1

CHAPTER TWO

BALANCE IS BULLSHIT

*When you say yes to others, make sure
you are not saying no to yourself.*

—Paulo Coelho, best-selling author of *The Alchemist*

*There is no such thing as work-life balance.
It is all life. The balance is within you.*

—Sadhguru Jaggi Vasudev, spiritual leader and yogi

I've asked quite a number of leaders whether there is such a thing as work-life balance. Almost everyone says no without hesitation. They agree there are times we're present, we're grounded, we're in sync with what matters, and we're in the zone—feeling all the joyous personal and professional satisfaction we're looking for. Yet, it's as though the second we become aware of it, the experience disappears. Additionally, balance looks different for every individual. For most leaders, balance becomes work-life integration, with the ability to work at any time while having flexibility for family and personal activities throughout the day. Most leaders I know take this path: they bring their work home and bring their home to work.

It's easier for most of us to recognize when we're out of sync because when we're too far off kilter, we feel it. The moment you recognize it, say to yourself, "Wait a second, let me slow down," stop, breathe, and address it directly. Ask yourself what you need to let go of, what you need to say no to, what you need to start or stop doing so you can get back in sync right now.

When you're out of sync, there's a choice to make. Like most people, I have an inordinate number of things I believe I *should* be doing to be a good friend, to be a good sister, to be a good daughter in law, to be a good mom, to be a good businesswoman, to be a good wife. We all have competing priorities, and we need practices to help us pause to say, "Yes, it can all be done, just not all at once. You can have it all, just not all at the same time."

STOP AND BREATHE

Have you ever regretted saying yes to something? I sure have. Several years ago, I registered fifteen months in advance for a five-day physical/mental/emotional endurance challenge. When it came time to participate in the program, I was in the worst physical condition of my life. My mom had Alzheimer's and was living with me every other weekend; I was cooking a very specialized diet for my dad; my son's father had checked out and offered no co-parenting help; my husband (at the time) was not very supportive; and I was running two businesses. I was taking care of everyone and everything but myself.

I had signed up for this program before we discovered my mom had Alzheimer's. It was an expensive use-it-or-lose-it thing. Everything logical inside me told me not to go, but I was encouraged by friends who assured me that I could always opt to do nothing and just relax. At the very least it meant getting away and gaining some much-needed perspective on my life.

Our days began at 5:00 a.m. and ended at 2:00 a.m. and the program consisted of an array of physical and mental challenges, ranging from walking on hot coals to self-defense—so much for rest! Of many incredible events, the most memorable day was when I climbed five mountain peaks with a team. We were being timed to get our team up and back down in a four-hour period or less, with the added challenge of building a sculpture at the top with bricks and wood we carried up ourselves.

I've been an athlete my entire life and, because I have exercise-induced asthma, I brought my inhaler and figured I'd be fine. From our team of fifty people, we each had to choose a buddy. To my delight, I was chosen by a woman bodybuilder, who said she'd picked me because she had seen my mental toughness. I felt as if I'd paired with the best buddy ever, because there was no way this woman would fail. We self-assuredly loaded up our backpacks, certain we'd be the first ones to the top. I'd led plenty of ropes courses and leadership exercises throughout my career and I was brimming with confidence.

We were already in the mountains, but as we gained altitude, breathing became difficult, causing me to stop more and more frequently to catch my breath. My overly fit partner was becoming frustrated. The rules of the game required us to be paired; you could trade partners, but you couldn't be solo. Things weren't getting better—with my pace or her attitude. Finally, I gasped, "You need a new partner. Just grab somebody else and I'll take whoever their partner is."

The switch was made and we both felt instant relief. I ended up with this cherubic eighteen-year-old young man who was the textbook definition of positivity. Every ten steps he told me, "You're doing great. You can do this!" After about twenty minutes, I wanted to kill him. He was a lovely young man, but I didn't need encouragement; I needed air. I couldn't will my way through it. I had to take it one step at a time, slow down, *stop, and breathe.*

PRACTICES FOR SUCCESS

Feeling Out of Balance? Stop and Breathe

While the illusion of balance in our external lives may be just that—an illusion—we can foster internal balance and move toward emotional equilibrium that will help us cope with the challenges life offers. We don't clearly see that our interpretations dictate how we experience the world and our place in it—and we just go along for the ride with whatever emotional reaction we have when, instead, we could ask ourselves, "Wait a second, are these thoughts even true? Am I seeing things as they are, or am I reacting to something that's happened in the past?" Often our external responses to challenges are based on things we've internalized that have no real basis in fact—and those "things" can be negative and self-defeating, challenging our internal sense of peace and groundedness.

When I catch myself reacting, I stop and ask, "What am I telling myself? Is it true, or is it head trash?" This helps me unravel what's factual from a kneejerk emotional response based in fear. I've gotten better at recognizing when I'm reacting to something, and before my mouth or emotions engage, I've learned to pause and check in with myself.

When it isn't working, I sort out what the facts are and, if need be, write a new story to elicit a better response. During that pause, I stop and breathe until I find my internal balance again.

When I told my buddy I needed to "stop and breathe," a light bulb went on in my head: this was *exactly* what I needed to do in my life, a perfect metaphor. It was the life lesson I needed to learn: the lesson that balance is bullshit. It's a matter of figuring out what to say yes and no to while making space for yourself in the process. I surrendered that day, and on the mountain I paused after every twenty steps to "stop and breathe."

My superhero buddy carried my backpack and all our bricks to make it easier for me. We got to the top and built our structure. I was light-headed and really struggling; I had to get back down that mountain as soon as possible. As he and I hiked down, I learned about his parents' divorce and the difficulties in his young life, despite his mask of positivity. As we descended, I began to feel exhilarated. My lungs were back at full capacity and we ended up running across the finish line. And we made it to the top, thanks to my buddy.

At the bottom of the mountain, I reunited with my first partner. She felt bad about leaving me and we had a very honest conversation in which she admitted she didn't do well when people couldn't perform even though she realized there was nothing I could have done about it.

Life handed me exactly what I needed to learn from my two partners: the first of whom was very tough mentally and physically and a great leader, yet not a great teammate. My second partner was an angelic young man who was caring and determined to be there with me, no matter what. He was the perfect teammate. He helped me and he carried the load. Though I thought I was doing nothing, he told me *I* helped *him* by simply listening to his challenges in life—and not *doing* a thing. I needed both lessons to correct my imbalanced life at home. That day changed the course of my life.

The experience was the perfect metaphor for what happens when we're overcommitted and feeling imbalanced. We have to take a hard look at what's in front of us and stop doing things that aren't working. It means learning to say no and learning to contribute by being a team player, not always the leader. You make space for others to contribute *and* it lightens the load.

You can't always *make* things happen, and you can't do it all. At times you have to let someone guide you, let go, and let others take the lead. Finding balance is a matter of saying yes and no to what fulfills you and your life without overcommitting. When life happens, you stop and breathe, gain perspective, gather your teammates and proceed forward. It's a continual dance.

MAXIMIZE SUCCESS

Becky Roloff

Becky is the embodiment of what it means to lead well. Yes, she's an accomplished professional with a Harvard MBA, yet her simple wisdom stems from her parents and her humble upbringing in North Dakota. Her moral compass, common sense, and can-do attitude help her keep her internal balance when the world around her is out of whack. She shared a few of her core beliefs with me in an interview, and these were among my favorites:

"First get the car out of the ditch." Becky's father owned a gas station, and this was his metaphor. "If your car's in the ditch, the first step should always be to get the car out of the ditch. Only after it is out of the ditch should you then figure out how the car got into the ditch. Last, you need to ensure the car never goes into the ditch again. You must proceed with problem solving in that order; it keeps you from blaming others. If the car is still in the ditch, it doesn't matter what caused it or how to prevent it; the car's still in the ditch."

"Every decision will have eighty-three problems, so pick your best set." Determine what set of problems will move you forward, and anticipate them so you can prepare. This helps manage expectations because even the best solution will create problems.

Martyrdom is overrated. Keeping our internal balance starts with good self-care: Becky says that she has zero tolerance for martyrs, believing that you must first take care of yourself to keep yourself strong before you can take care of others and keep your bucket full. "Look good, feel good, do good; it's not a selfish act to take care of yourself."

"There's no such thing as balance. I think you have to take responsibility for your own life and we all find time for the things we care about. Take responsibility and accept the eighty-three problems that come with your choices."

THE PRICE OF YES

Prioritization means we need to say no to things. When someone asks you if you want to do something, do you have a hard time saying no, even if it means rearranging your existing plans? For most of us, when we say no, it's inevitably followed by a long explanation because we're feeling guilty. Many years ago, during a program I was participating in, we were asked to invent a new practice, and I thought, *I can't do one more thing right now*. I had so much on my plate personally and professionally I couldn't see a way to add another thing. So I invented a practice to decline new commitments, which was about learning to say no. It ended up being really tough; my kneejerk response when asked to do things is to say yes because I really enjoy new things and it's automatic for me. The trouble with saying yes to something is that, often, it isn't just one yes; it's a whole cascade of yesses you're committing to without realizing it.

Using the format I've included here, I tasked myself to practice saying no and failed miserably for a long time. Very rarely could I just say, "No thank you," and stop talking; it was always, "No and here are the forty-two reasons I'm saying no." Blocking that tendency to overexplain is something I'm still challenged with. Sometimes, I just don't want to do a particular thing—and that's enough.

PRACTICES FOR SUCCESS

Learning to Say No

Every time you say yes to something, you're also saying yes to much, much more—but how often do you stop to consider all that your first yes entails in terms of time, work, and commitment? Try this: When someone asks you to take on a new responsibility or job, don't be too quick to say yes. Instead, tell them you'll consider it and when you'll get back to them. Then take the time to sit down with a pad and pencil and list all those additional things you're taking on by saying yes. Take your time, and write them all down. If you look at your list and realize that all of those yesses add up to more than you're willing to commit to, you can say no with a clear conscience and without hesitating. If you're determined to find balance in your life between what you must do, versus what others would like you to do, this is a powerful place to start.

Learning to say no—and to stick with it—is always going to be a work in progress, because we're so used to saying yes—and yes, that includes me (my company is named YESS!, which explains a lot about me).

A good example of this is hosting the holidays. In my mind, these holiday gatherings would be like something from a greeting card: family and friends together, everyone in harmony. Somehow, every holiday I hosted wasn't anything close to that utopian experience for me. My guests seemed to love it, yet I was exhausted, disappointed, and resentful. Why?

I started to unpack it by counting up all the unacknowledged yesses my first yes included: If I said yes to hosting the holiday, it also meant getting the kids to clean their rooms, cleaning the house, going to the grocery store and planning the menu, and finding all these really lovely recipes I would never make again—because for some reason at Thanksgiving, I'm suddenly Julia Child, so I inevitably opt to do something spectacular. This whole litany of labors—

preparing my home, organizing my kitchen, getting the new do-dads and place-card holders and dishes so our home resembled a magazine spread—all of it was supposed to create something wonderful, but it became stressful because all those yesses were added and *nothing was removed from my calendar.*

Nothing came off my plate to create space for all of those yesses. Other things—like working out, reading, spending time with friends, or enjoying the experience of prepping for it all—went out the window because of things I *had* to do, such as run my two businesses. Now, before I say yes, I begin by making a list of all the ancillary yesses that first yes commits me to. I still say yes, but it's more intentional. This practice forces me to acknowledge what I'm agreeing to and choose accordingly. When I started looking for work-arounds for the parts I didn't enjoy—such as shopping—I discovered that I could order the basics of my meal online and focus on the "trimmings" and getting my house ready. I could still doctor up the Thanksgiving turkey and add family recipes—and that's how I do it now. This has become a great solution and has helped me realize that letting go of my expectations are the key to having it all.

The first year I tried this new method, I sheepishly told my mother, "This is probably going to disappoint you, but I used one of those grocery services and preordered the bird." She said, "I wish I'd done that!" She then called her sisters who echoed her enthusiasm. I felt as though I'd received a get-out-of-jail free card from the whole "turkey business" and sprung my mom and aunts to boot! It was all due to the practice of learning to say no and asking myself, "Do I really enjoy doing all of this, or just parts of it, and what can I do to help me get my day-to-day life back in balance?" So how do you use this in your life at home and work?

Delegate and Elevate™

Our lives are so fraught with demands; family, work, and relationships all make claims on our time and pull us in multiple directions. In addition, the simple practicalities of life also have to be addressed—and statistically, we know that women are the ones who are most often tasked with taking care of things on the home front. How is it possible to find balance when you're being pulled in multiple directions at once? The first step is identifying and ridding your schedule of those things you don't like or aren't good at so you have the space you need to do more of what you love. A useful exercise is Delegate and Elevate", used here with the kind permission of its creator, Gino Wickman, the founder of EOS Worldwide, of which I am a Certified EOS Implementer™, helping leaders implement tools like this and much more.

The idea is to delegate everything from the bottom quadrants as quickly as you can do it well and revisit the tool and exercise whenever you're feeling you don't have the time you need to do great work with free time for family and other passions. As a result, you'll be doing what you love and are great at, and your life will become richer, fuller, and more meaningful. In my experience, it really works!

DELEGATE AND ELEVATE™ QUADRANTS

QUADRANT 1: "LOVE/GREAT"

Activities are those that you've mastered, that you love doing, that give you energy and a sense of fulfillment.

QUADRANT 2: "LIKE/GOOD"

Activities are those that you can do with minimal effort and that give you enjoyment and satisfaction.

QUADRANT 3: "DON'T LIKE/GOOD"

Activities are those that you are good at doing—you have learned to do them well through repetition and necessity—but they don't give you a real satisfaction or a sense of fulfillment.

QUADRANT 4: "DON'T LIKE/NOT GOOD"

Activities are most likely outside your area of expertise and leave you feeling inadequate and frustrated.

HANGING ON TO WHAT MATTERS: VALUES DRIVING PRIORITIES

The one place we need consistency is in living our values. When we're coming from our values, we spend our time doing what matters and we're at our best. When we're misaligned with our values, life doesn't work, we're out of sync, and we feel uncomfortable. One way to keep your priorities aligned with your values is through the practice of calendaring.

PRACTICES FOR SUCCESS

Calendaring

What matters most to you? Does the way you spend your time reflect your priorities? This exercise will help you to put your concentration into the areas of your life that are most important to you.

1. List the three to five areas in your life that are critical to your happiness. They might include family, health, career, spirituality, community, relationships, learning, and recreation, but they can be anything, as long as they are priorities for you.

2. Next, take a blank set of calendar pages and jot down your vision of an ideally balanced life. Imagine it. Don't edit, just set up a life you'd wake up to every day, excited to live.

3. Now, print out your actual calendar for the same number of months you used for your "ideal" calendar in step 2 and compare the two calendars. How does what you *actually* do on a day-to-day basis compare with your "ideal" calendar? Where are the biggest gaps? What's included? What's excluded?

4. Write down the first step you need to take to realize a life that is more reflective of your "ideal" calendar.

5. Begin immediately; especially if you find your ideal and reality are worlds apart.

The word *balance* is bantered about in self-help books and health magazines all the time, as if it's a destination we are all seeking. Yet I haven't met anyone who lives there. It's an illusion, and we need to give up the pursuit of such an unrealistic Zen where all areas of our life are in perfect equilibrium. It's not that it doesn't exist; it's fleeting, often accidental, and definitely impermanent. Simply said, we visit that impeccable state, realize it—and life happens. The Zen slips just beyond our fingertips again. The trick is defining what balance means for *you*. Visiting that Zen more consistently means learning to slow down, intentionally *choosing* what to say yes and no to, based on your values, and delegating what you don't enjoy and aren't good at, while spending more time doing what you love and are great at. Simple? Yes. Easy? No.

For bonus information, practices, and resources:
www.ChasingPerfection.net/book/chapter-2

CHAPTER THREE

PUT ON YOUR OXYGEN MASK FIRST

*If your compassion does not include
yourself, then it is incomplete.*

—Jack Kornfield, author

*Self-care is never a selfish act. It is simply good
stewardship of the only gift I have, the gift I
was put on this Earth to offer to others.*

—Parker Palmer, speaker, educator, and activist

It's easy to fall into the habit of putting yourself last. Especially during the sandwich years, when your kids and parents both need help from you. We're working so hard to be everywhere, for everyone who needs us—for everyone *except* us.

Sleep, exercise, and what you consume are critical to your physical and mental health. Do you make time for self-care in your life? Or are you, like so many people, too engaged in doing for others to do for yourself? Do yourself a favor—and also do a favor for those whom you love and who count on you: take care of yourself first before you spread yourself too thin helping others. As flight attendants advise, put on your oxygen mask first before assisting others.

How do you manage it all when your life seems to be running you rather than the other way around? If you're fortunate enough to have a great partner, that's a tremendous help. So is having a network of support at home and at work. Making time for fun is part of healthy self-care as well—defining your passions and finding and pursuing hobbies for yourself. Otherwise, you're on an ever-turning hamster wheel of work and commitments. Resentment toward everyone and everything can occur if you're not determined. The most powerful thing to change is your thinking. You shift from "I can't do it all!" to "How can I succeed?" Reframing how you think about things will change how your world appears and, ultimately, what's possible.

When it came to my commitments—work, aging parents, kids, home, relationships—I was always the last one on my list, and the first one I would steal time from. When chaos happened, there was little left over for me: no time, no energy, and on top of that, self-criticism for failing to take better care of myself. The first step forward was to change my thinking and eliminate negative messages, internally and externally. If I forgot and my self-criticism returned, I practiced asking myself, "Would you talk to anyone else this way? If not, stop it."

I began to take inventory of my relationships as well, including the quality of time spent with others. I decided that if it were draining or difficult to see someone, I would choose to not spend time with that person. I didn't have to enjoy time with everyone equally, and I didn't have to use what little energy I had to keep company with them. I left the option open to change my mind. I was truly choosing. Every choice I made was in response to whether I gained energy and felt better from taking that particular action. I acknowledged that I was firing only on one cylinder at that time, and I chose to not expend energy unless I spent it on something that moved me forward. I was determined to adjust all my thinking to the positive. I stopped watching the news; I chose to watch only funny or uplifting movies. *Everything* I chose to do had to move me in some way toward becoming happier and healthier.

I didn't have a significant other at the time; I was going through my second divorce, and I was putting a lot of thought into what defined a successful partnership. I looked at it from a significant-other angle, a business angle, and a familial angle. At one point I believed I might never have a significant-other relationship again and wondered how, if that were the case, I would make my life joyful, peaceful, and truly fulfilled every day.

I didn't want to publicly admit I was going through a second divorce, because I felt embarrassed. My first marriage had been abusive; my second marriage had dissolved from neglect and non-communication. I took a very hardcore look at myself. I believed that making a mistake once was forgivable, but when it became a recurring situation in which I was the common denominator, I knew I had work to do.

I was trying to maintain my businesses and income, to be a decent mom, to be a dutiful daughter and a good friend, to do all the right things. Yet I remember feeling like a fraud and a failure, because here I was, teaching people how to change their worldview, coaching them on how everything starts between your ears, and you have to develop the thinking, language, practices, and behaviors to support the life you desire. Yet, all I could think of relative to my life was that I sucked; I sucked in every domain of life.

CREATING HEALTHIER PRACTICES

Although I had told clients hundreds of times that when you change your practices, you'll change your life, it was only at this low point in my life that I fully understood those words. So they became my mantra. I focused on getting enough sleep, which didn't always come easily. I ate the healthiest food I could. I lowered the bar, knowing if I were to exercise at least once a week, progress would be made, and I could make exercise a social thing: a double win. I maintained my gym membership because, in my world, it served multiple purposes: I moved my body, I enjoyed it, and it gave me people to interact with. I needed their energy around me. So every day I went, I celebrated.

My celebrations always include music, which has consistently been a small but significant support for me. In my twenties I spent a lot of my time dancing in clubs because I loved the music, the energy, the movement, and the fun of it. I reawakened to dancing later in life when I started going to clubs again (although it was tough to find places where older people were!), and I discovered Zumba classes. My son introduced me to the joys of Wii fitness as it emerged. It was so much fun and also happened to be exercise I could do with my son. Dance Dance Revolution and Rock Band were fun for both of us and moved the needle on my sense of taking care of myself.

I knew if I could find gratitude every day, it would move me out of my sad state, so I began keeping a daily gratitude journal. Every night before I slept, I wrote down ten to twelve things I was grateful for. Sometimes, all I could come up with was, "It was seventy and sunny today," and then I'd sit and wonder what else had been great that day and realize I could include the fact that my mom was still with me, even in her advanced state of Alzheimer's. I would work myself through my practice one item at a time. If you were to ask me today, I could rattle off two hundred things I feel blessed and grateful for, but during that darker time, it required daily practice to open up my mind to the infinite blessings I enjoyed. Every evening I told myself that things were better that day. I might not see it as a better day, I might not feel it, I might not always recognize it, but that day was better, and the next day would be even better. Over time, it became easier to believe each day was better than the previous one, and my gratitude journal provided the evidence.

This period of pain, loss, loneliness, challenges, and setbacks lasted about a year and a half for me. It wasn't unrelenting. There were some happy times, but then life would throw another curveball and sadness would overtake me like a wave because I was grieving over many things at once. I was guided by my determination about my future and the self-discipline I exerted to maintain my daily practices. I had to look at what I was doing, question my choices, and weigh them based on whether they were moving me forward or limiting me.

I had to rediscover what I enjoyed doing. I'm a doer by nature, so it was a big step for me to pause and ask myself whether I liked who I was, what I enjoyed, and whether I could be alone with myself without the distraction of a hundred things to do and plan.

MAXIMIZE SUCCESS

Susan Denk

Putting on our oxygen mask requires us to change our habits and embrace taking care of ourselves—and addiction is one of the toughest challenges to overcome. I've had the pleasure of knowing Susan Denk, the owner of White Crane Construction, for many years. One thing rings true in all areas of Susan's life, and that is her tenacity. She brings her tenacity to White Crane, the extensive service work she does through the YWCA and the Women's Foundation of Minnesota, and also her sobriety. Susan opens up about addiction to shed light on its stigma—and her path back to self-care and good health, central to putting on your oxygen mask first.

Now that she has been sober for over twenty-five years, Susan can reflect on her life and see where her turning points were. Although neither of her parents struggle with addiction, they did pass on this genetic predisposition and "silent killer" to Susan. Growing up in a structured household helped keep Susan in line during her young adult years, but as she grew older, she began to foster her addiction. "I had a big job and a strong personal relationship, which meant lots of fun, lots of dinner parties, lots of wine. All of the trappings, if you will, of success." Regardless of how it looked on the outside, however, Susan knew she "didn't drink like other people," and was very moved when she'd meet people in recovery and hear their story. "You look at those people and think, *Wow! They have a great life and are sober.* They hold a mirror up and you know there's hope." Now that she is sober herself, Susan enjoys being that mirror for others.

Susan is grateful to have sobriety guide her life, and when asked what her best practice is, she shares that it's her AA and Alanon meetings. Regularly attending meetings gives Susan the opportunity to "reboot and get back to a spiritual core," which allows her to keep her sobriety without much difficulty. Susan also considers carefully those who she surrounds herself with. "I am careful to surround myself with people in recovery or who understand the seriousness of addiction," she says. "There are so many still struggling with addiction and mental illness that having a healthy core group of friends allows those still struggling to see there is another way to pursue a happy and meaningful life." As I said earlier, when you change your practices, you'll change your life!

INTO THE LIGHT

I came out of that year and a half a better, happier, wiser person. My life improved after overcoming my rock bottom and cleaning house. I released the thinking, people, practices, and beliefs that didn't move me forward or fit any longer, and I replaced them with things that did. This resulted in increased clarity, passion, and energy.

MAXIMIZE SUCCESS

Anita Janssen

Anita Janssen founded her first company right out of college and has been a risk-taking serial entrepreneur ever since. A champion equestrienne who competes nationally in cutting horse events, she comes across as supremely competent and cool-headed. What few people know about her is her long-term struggle with crippling anxiety:

It's the most overwhelming feeling I have ever experienced, to the point where it manifests physical responses. It becomes a vicious circle, because I start to feel the anxiety rise, and then my chest gets heavy, my heart beats fast, and I get crazy hot, like I am cooking from the inside out. Just knowing those sensations are coming only adds to my anxiety.

Anxiety is not something I live with 100 percent of the time, which is a blessing. I haven't come up with any great rhyme or reason as to why I will go through periods of time without having it. I'll have stuff flying at me from different directions and be handling it. It's all good and then—boom!—it hits.

I have learned anxiety is a chemical issue and that I need to reset the chemistry in my body. I've been on and off anxiety meds throughout my life. I am very clear my two triggers are (1) not knowing and (2) financial anxiety. That first one has made me relentless in pursuit of answers. I think it has actually served me well in business, and maybe even life, because if there's something going on, I want to get to the bottom of it, and I am going to get there faster than most people will because it is literally driving me crazy. Once I get to the bottom of it, I get some peace—but sometimes that's not an easy journey.

One of the most empowering practices for dealing with my anxiety was when I became a member of a women's executive group. At one of our first meetings, there was a discussion about how many of us were on anti-depressants or anti-anxiety meds, and I was stunned: This was a group of women who have accomplished amazing things, running successful multimillion-dollar businesses like me, and they had the same issues going on that I did! I thought I was alone. Since that time,

I've been really aware of this problem in dealing with leaders who are highly productive, are highly success- ful, and are movers and shakers, because a majority of those I know will tell you they struggle with anxiety. It's made me question whether there is some link between whatever it is that fuels our anxiety and whatever it is that fuels entrepreneurs to be successful. I have no idea if that bridge exists, but I know anxiety exists, and many of those I know who have anxiety are people I consider to be some of the most amazing, successful, put-together, kickass leaders in my world.

I've learned when things are overly complex, you can't always think your way to better acting, but you *can* act your way to better thinking. After I lowered the bar and became more active, my thinking gradually shifted to the positive. I was following through, keeping my promises to myself. The more I did it, the more I believed I could count on myself again, and I felt better because I was doing the things that helped me. People helped me: my friends stepped up and lovingly nagged me into getting out of the house. My brothers stepped in and helped with my parents' care and it didn't feel as if it were all on my shoulders. I figured out what worked for me and when—meditation and exercise in the morning and gratitude journal at night—and I made sure they happened.

PRACTICES FOR SUCCESS

Exercise

When we're already overloaded and stressed, the idea of adding exercise to an overly busy life can seem impossible. In this case, I'm an advocate for lowering the bar, because some exercise is better than *no* exercise. When my world fell apart, the thought of working out several times a week was overwhelming. The thought of anything additional, really, was overwhelming. So I lowered the bar for myself. I figured that if I could get to the gym even once a week, it was a win and something I was doing just for me.

Think about what it takes to get you moving. Are you someone who needs someone else to join you in exercising, or is exercise more of a solitary practice? Do you like teams, or machines, or classes? A walk with a good friend is exercise and fills you up in other ways at the same time. When I was at my rock bottom, exercise moved me forward even if I wasn't doing well overall. My life changed; it was a series of small, consistent, incremental improvements that became a habit rather than a big, sweeping change. It was about taking one step forward, every day. We all have complex times in our lives when we need to simplify things and take the next step. Once we do, we can take another step and repeat the process over time. It's about progress, not perfection.

If you're taking care of everyone before you care for yourself, stop now or you'll hit rock bottom and be forced to stop. Take stock of what you need to reset your thinking and practices to become the best version of yourself. These are the essential practices for every day that will also be your first recourse when life is off track. As the airlines advise, if the cabin's pressure drops, put on your oxygen mask first before assisting others.

For bonus information, practices, and resources:
www.ChasingPerfection.net/book/chapter-3

CHAPTER FOUR

CONQUERING CATASTROPHE

It ain't how hard you hit; it's about how hard you can get
hit and keep moving forward. How much you can take
and keep moving forward. That's how winning is done.

—Sylvester Stallone as boxer Rocky
Balboa in the 1976 film *Rocky*

Rock bottom became the solid foundation
upon which I rebuilt my life.

—J. K. Rowling, best-selling author of the *Harry Potter* series

When the bottom's falling out of your life, what do you do? Do you stop working? Stop caring for your children? Stop getting out of bed?

No. What you *must* do is to learn to let go. It's like being strapped into a nightmarish roller coaster: you don't have much say over what's happening. All you can do is go along for the awful ride and do your best to manage your own thinking and behavior.

What are some of the things that can pull the rug out from under us? Health is the big one: your own or that of your loved ones. It could be a business partner who lets you down. It could be your spouse or your significant other. It could be that your family is broken from divorce. I have a good friend who's been through some big personal challenges, a CEO with a billion-dollar business, who told me, "Throw anything at me; I can take any business challenge. Yet if something happens to my family, it's another story; it stops me. Everything other than family, it's just stuff to manage."

For me, it was a toxic mix of my parents' declining health, my second divorce, the loss of my home, having to move suddenly, the recession, and financial worries. I felt emotionally hijacked and wrung out from all the feelings I was having: overwhelmed, over-loaded, and mired in grief and loss. Yet life didn't stop; I still had to deal with it and keep moving forward, even though I felt incapable of getting anything done. I started to let go of the little things, and the chaos began. I dug deep and kept going because people I loved were counting on me—and I remember wondering if I'd ever get my mojo back. Usually, I have boundless energy; I'm motivated and excited about life. With all my challenges occurring at the same time, I wondered how I could get through even one day. Could I manage to at least take a shower?

I discovered most people don't know how to have a vulner-able conversation any more than I did without prompting from my WPO chapter chair roundtable group. Frankly, they don't want to think about it, because it's uncomfortable for everyone; catastrophic situations are scary. I understand. I was the last person to bring my troubles up, because I didn't want to be a burden or a bore. Yet it's hard when you're *that* person because you need somewhere to vent and gain clarity in your daily life. Talking about personal problems often needs the encouragement of a coach or a therapist, who can be incredibly valuable at these times.

As challenging as my life was, it also became much simpler. All the things I'd normally worry about, the minor distractions that ordinarily consumed my thinking, receded into the distance when my needs became as simple as wanting to hug my son, wanting to be happy with what I had, and wanting to spend time with the people who mattered to me, especially those whom I was aware I was losing. I wanted to live every day with no regrets. Every day, I'd rest my head on the pillow and ask myself whether there was anything I regretted that day. If I thought of anything, I'd ask myself what I was going to do about it. If my regret for the day was not having called my mom one more time, or not having visited someone, I began my day by doing just that. When I started doing something about my regrets, I learned to appreciate what I *had*, and peace followed.

The unexpected gift we get when we're dealing with big things is the clarity we have when we're pared down to life's essentials. It's actually very peaceful because you have far less manufactured stress. You learn to face your new reality accepting that you can't control everything, but you can make the best of what you're dealing with right now. As trivial distractions fall away, you realize they are the small things you spend your energy on and they're not worth it.

I think it's very helpful to write down your thoughts about what you're experiencing and to see on paper your patterns of thinking, because thoughts always precede feelings. Do you realize your thinking produces your feelings? Your power is in changing your thinking. Most of us live at the whim of our feelings. Like a shirt clipped to a clothesline, the wind comes and blows us in all directions. People feel sad and think they're stuck there, rather than questioning how what they believe is causing them to feel sad. Knowing how to reframe your thinking is a bridge to shifting your experience in the world.

PRACTICES FOR SUCCESS

Take One Small Action and Write Down the Win

When you're at the top of your game and feeling great, you take small wins for granted. When your life is upended, it seems to be very short on wins and it helps us to count even the smallest ones and to acknowledge and record them. When it's all you can do to get out of bed, and you *do* get out of bed, that's a win. If you accomplish something, large or small, write it down. Did you put away the laundry? Good job. Did you manage to fit in a visit to the dentist? Congrats. Did you work in the garden or just sit on the porch and close your eyes in the sunshine—whatever small step you took toward normalcy, write it down and hold on to the feeling you had at that moment. Otherwise, you have no record. Your brain can be a funny little trap: when you're feeling lost, you'll tell yourself that you accomplished nothing the previous week, but having thirty things written down stops you from *believing* that nothing was accomplished. Your notes are the evidence those things happened; you did them. It's progress.

FOCUS ON WHAT MATTERS

As I'm writing this, I'm thinking about a cousin of mine who's sixty-five and going to die in the next few weeks. The sad part is he hated his job for much of his life; he was miserable in it for years and finally quit about a year ago. Shortly after he quit, he found out he had cancer and was immediately submerged into months of difficult treatment that, ultimately, hasn't been successful. For five months, he and his family made time to do all the things they'd put off, but he told my brother, "I wish I hadn't waited sixty-four years to do all we'd dreamed because now it's *real*. Now all the 'I love yous' come out, along with all of the 'Why didn't we do the things we talked about doing earlier? Why did we waste all this time making other things more important?'"

"I'll go to my grave being fulfilled," he continued, "but I could've lived this way every day of my life. Instead, I worried about all this meaningless stuff rather than appreciating right now and doing the things that mattered." Now, "right now" was all he had.

When you're thrown into catastrophe, being present is one of the gifts you receive because that's all you can be—present. You can't live for tomorrow, because you don't know how many tomorrows you have. And you can't be in the past, because all that does is dredge up regret and you can't change it. You have to be right where you are, asking yourself what you can do at this moment.

Most of us have the luxury of making up problems and worrying about what might happen, or about what other people think, or how it should be, or how we compare to others—but honestly? It's bullshit. We're missing life while it's happening. When the bottom falls out, all we have is right now. And when you live in the moment, it's actually very peaceful, and it gives you choice. It doesn't matter what you did yesterday. I can't worry about what I might do for my cousin three weeks from now, because he won't be here. I can choose to be in the present and be glad I took the time to call him to say, "I want you to know how deeply I care and though I may not have seen you much, I love you. I love you fully in this moment."

Rhoda Olsen

It took courage for Great Clips CEO Rhoda Olsen to stand up in front of a convention hall and admit, "My father was an abusive alcoholic, my mother was suicidal; I had to take my prom date to the locked psych ward; my son is an alcoholic and a drug addict, and my other son battled depression." But she did, and she's glad she put down the mask of perfection and shared her humanity because, she says, "All of a sudden everybody in the audience had permission to say, 'My life is kind of messed up too, but it's not going to hold me back.'"

Yes, she's a successful businesswoman who survived cancer among other personal challenges, but "People look at me and imagine that because I'm successful, I've got a perfect life. They're wrong. Nobody has a perfect life. The perfect lives we see on Facebook are made up. People don't want to admit it, but everybody's life is full of pain and difficulty. Real life is messy, and for people to believe someone has something different than that and accept that as a goal is what drives people to feel they're being short-changed. I think women in particular perpetuate that notion. I don't know why, but it seems like women believe they have to make up their life as really good when it's not—and then we all try to strive for that when no one has it. It's stupid." Rhoda doesn't let herself get bogged down by challenges. She determined what she could do to move forward and kept doing it. She's a forward-looking person who rarely thinks back on unhappy or painful events, and that attitude has served her well in dealing with illness and other challenges.

Rhoda's willingness to be vulnerable allowed her employees to be more open with each other, too, leading to better relationships and creating a caring culture with increased productivity.

We live in the illusion that the future is something we can predict, when it really isn't. We also have a need to plan. As my mom used to say, "Pray as if it's up to God. Act as if it's up to you." You have to remember your plan is an illusion. You plan, and life happens and throws your plan into the air and out the window. However, there are practices you can use to reclaim some sense of efficacy in your life. Every small positive step will take you in that direction. During times in my life when it seemed as if everything was beyond my control, I found goal setting helped me to focus on the future while taking steps forward to get my life back on track.

PRACTICES FOR SUCCESS

Goal Setting

Goal setting is important when life is overwhelming us. We need to scale our goals realistically and not make them into something else, adding to our stress. When goal setting, we often saddle ourselves with an impossible ideal and wind up blaming ourselves when we fail to meet it. Our small wins add up to big ones when we're keeping score, and they can help move us out of the state of stuckness catastrophe pitches us into. Documenting our wins and putting them somewhere we'll see every day will remind us of our victories.

Maybe our goal is to take a walk twice a week; maybe it's to cook a healthy meal once a week. When we can see we've actually achieved our goal, we can pause and celebrate for a moment. ("I'm doing all right. That's what I was trying to accomplish.") Once we have a pattern of success, we can move our goals up or add others, which lets us strive and succeed while building our confidence, because every time we reach a goal, we're winning.

WHEN A FRIEND IS IN TROUBLE, HOW CAN YOU HELP?

Just as we have our own difficulties, so do the other people in our lives. We may want to help them, but it can be challenging to know how to be most helpful to someone who's going through a crisis. People say things they think sound sensible and even compassionate, but when you're the one in crisis, these remarks can seem clichéd at best and hurtful at worst. I'm absolutely one of those people who has bumbled in plenty of situations, and I likely will again—but I've got a better handle on it now than I used to.

When people are dealing with grief and loss, it's a process, and nobody does it the same way. Interestingly, our culture isn't very tolerant of the grieving process; we tend to think people ought to get over it, as though there's a time limit on how long it should take to get past anger, pain, and sadness. I learned quickly when I was in the midst of my grief that the best people for me to be with were those who'd had similar experiences and were able to relate without judging.

Sometimes, when we want to help, we'll tell friends to call us if they need anything. But the last thing a person in this state can do is call someone for help. One of the least helpful things you can say is, "Please reach out if there's anything I can do" or "Just ask. I'm there," because people in pain are not usually going to ask; they can't. Imagine someone in a state of grief picking up the phone to say, "Hey, could you make my family dinner? Oh, could you come over and do my laundry? Could you do the grocery shopping? Could you walk my dog? Could you pick up my kids? Could you give me a ride to my chemo appointment and sit with me?" That's just not how it works. Yes, the person making the offer means well. There's nothing malicious about it, but there's also nothing helpful about it, because a person in pain usually can't and won't ask.

THE BEST THING YOU CAN DO
IS JUST *DO SOMETHING*

When I lost my mother, some friends showed up at my house with bags of groceries, unasked and unexpectedly. It was so helpful, so thoughtful. I'd been feeling bad because people were stopping over and I hadn't any food in the house, and the last thing I was thinking about was going to the grocery store when I was in the midst of making funeral arrangements, calling family and friends, trying to pull together family photos for a slideshow, and all the rest of the details accompanying the loss that were cascading in on me.

How can you help? By saying, "What do you have this week? I'm free Wednesday. I'm coming over from ten to two, and I'll do anything you need. I'll be at your house." People in pain usually make polite noises about not putting you out, but you must just press on: "You know what? I'll just stop by." Bringing food is always a great option. Ask people to make a list, or work with their significant other if they have one, and ask, "What are the ten things I could do?" or "I don't have a chunk of time during the day, but tonight I can run some errands."

When my friend had cancer, before all the great scheduling apps were created, I created a calendar outlining when people could deliver meals for her family and invited everyone I knew to participate—some people didn't even know her. Everybody pitched in because it was organized and the calendar allowed everyone to know when it was their night—it didn't matter if they cooked a lavish meal or brought pizza as long as it was delivered as promised. If you're too far away to help, send a card saying you're thinking of that person, because it's a way to let them know there are people out there on their team, sending prayers and loving thoughts. And don't forget the caretaking family members because they are likely to deflect all the caring to the person who's ill, but as caretakers they are struggling too. Act, don't ask. Do, don't think.

GETTING THROUGH AN ILLNESS OR LOSS IS A JOURNEY, NOT A PIT STOP

We have a very short attention span when it comes to others' grief and health. While someone's in the middle of chemo and radiation, it's easy to be there for that person. But during the day-to-day living over the next year or more, after the immediate crisis is over, that person is still wondering, *Am I going to be okay*? Having someone to talk with continues to be very important. Maybe she seems fine because she's gone back to work. But after several days on the job, one day, she can hardly get out of bed; she feels like a failure, and it's scary. She's wondering if she'll ever be back to "normal" again, and those who supported her have moved on because she's back to work and they assume she's fine, the worst is over. Well, that's not the case for most people battling serious illness.

Don't assume, and don't expect. The road back from serious illness is a journey, and marginalizing a person's feelings by assuming they are on some kind of wellness timetable can undermine their already fragile health and self-esteem. You may need to check in, double down, and see what's really going on over time. It may surprise you.

MAXIMIZE SUCCESS

Amy Ronneberg

Amy Ronnegerg is amazing. She is a cancer survivor, a mother, and president of Be the Match, a multibillion-dollar nonprofit that oversees the largest bone-marrow registry program in the world. Amy talks candidly about the challenges on her path to health:

Cancer taught me a lot. Suddenly life becomes all about, "How do I be happy? How do I live the life I want to live, and keep my focus on the good and on my children? Do I love what I do every day?"

Through the surgeries, you're just fighting to get through the days. You're so sick and there are so many doctors' appointments. But then, once you start to get on the other side of the chemo, there's the exhaustion for another year or two, which nobody really warns you about. I was just tired all the time. But the worst of it was thinking about my kids. If I didn't make it, my three-year-old would have a few memories of me, but my one-year-old would have none. When my older girl turned five and I took her to kindergarten, I cried, wondering if I'd be there to take her sister when she was old enough for school.

Since I was a kid, I've always been driven. I was that girl in high school who was in every activity, and I had to have a 4.0 and be the best runner on the team. Then, suddenly, you get cancer and you're hearing about the survival rate for your illness—that only about 60 percent make it for five years—and it changes how you think. Now I focus on the good; on my children and loving what I do every day. I think I'm positive 99 percent of the time, but it's hard. You never stop expecting it to come back. Every time I wake up with an ache or pain, I'm praying to God not to make it be cancer. And even though I put it aside and keep moving forward, I know it's with me forever. That's true of everyone I've talked to who has had cancer.

I manage by compartmentalizing it, and I've gotten really good at just turning it off when it gets loud. When it's too loud to turn off, I have a conversation with another survivor or my oncologist. I'm more balanced than I used to be; when I'm home I'm not thinking about work, and I focus on the girls or what's in front of me. When I'm at work, I focus on the fact that I've got a team, and we can rely on each other. Cancer taught me how to leverage other people because I was not good at accepting help. It was really humbling to see the response when my

> friends organized our network to help me out. But after
> you're done with chemo, a lot of that falls away. People
> assume, "Oh she's got her hair back, she's over it," but the
> truth is it's still hard because the scary part sets in then.

It's similar with grief. When someone in your life passes, people around you will acknowledge your loss and grief for a short period, maybe three or four months. But grieving doesn't end, and sometimes it sneaks up on you and hits you as hard as it did at first. Several months after my father died, my daughter was singing in a choir concert, and they performed "Edelweiss." Even as I write this, I'm getting teary because that's the song my dad used to play for my mom, and it conjured up all those feelings again. I was holding back sobs at her concert. You never really get over it.

People beat themselves up: "Dammit, it's been a while, and I'm still grieving." But we shouldn't hold ourselves to anyone's arbitrary grieving agenda. I had a client whose relationship with her dad was central to her life. She was heartbroken when he died, and several months later, when one of her friends asked her, "It's been a while. How long are you going to hang onto this stuff?" her heart broke again. When we discussed it, I said, "You're going to hang onto it forever, and that's okay," and she started to bawl. She said, "I don't feel like I have permission to do that, because people are saying it's been too long."

What people don't understand is that grief is like losing a limb; it is a permanent thing. You can function without the limb, but it's never the same. You don't feel sad every day; you accept it over time, but there are moments when the grief returns and is powerfully visceral. Living grief is equally difficult; I've witnessed my kids suffering at family events as a result of divorce. When you have those moments, you need to give yourself permission to experience your emotions and be vulnerable in the moment. It's never logical or predictable; you ride the wave as it happens.

As compassionate as your grieving may have made you, other people will perceive loss differently from you. When a friend was telling me about dealing with her spouse's decline due to Alzheimer's, I related her experience to the experience I had with my mom: "It's so hard," I told her. She looked at me. "Losing your mom isn't the same as losing a spouse," she said. I realized she was right and apologized. Losing a beloved husband of forty years is an entirely different experience.

When you're in a compassionate place, though, you can respond tenderly with, "I can't imagine losing my partner or what it must be like for your life to unravel that way and to watch him go, because I watched my mom go, and it was awful, but she wasn't my partner, she was my parent. I'm so sorry this is happening and I understand this is an entirely different experience." Unfortunately, our culture doesn't provide much learning regarding how to endure grief or how to comfort those who are experiencing it. Here are some things you can do when you'd like to "do something."

WHEN CATASTROPHE HAPPENS

If You're the One Overwhelmed by Catastrophe:

- Celebrate what you do get done, not what you didn't.
- Allow others to help you if they offer.
- Don't be shy about asking for help, because people want to reach out but often don't know how to help; make a list and share it when asked.

- If you're feeling self-conscious and you need to talk to someone who won't judge or tell you to toughen up, find a coach or a therapist and unload.

- Let your process take as long as it needs to take. Don't let anyone put you on a timetable—not even yourself.

- Know that while grief never leaves you completely, it gets better in time. It really does.

If You Know Someone in This Situation, Remember...

- Don't say, "Call me if you need help or if you need to talk." Chances are the person in pain is too overwhelmed to make the effort. Be proactive: show up, do something. Basic life and home care is always needed.

- Offer to run errands. Help your friend to make a list, and take care of it yourself. Engage others to help as well.

- Bring food—and if you really want to help, organize other friends or relatives to do the same on a regular basis. In the midst of a crisis nobody has time to think about shopping or cooking—and they still have to eat.

- Does the person in pain have a dog? Walk it. Does that person have kids who play sports or have dance lessons? Get the schedule and drive them. Offer to babysit or take the kids to the park for the afternoon.

- If your friend has to have medical treatments such as chemo, drive them there and sit with them. Tell stories, laugh, hold hands. Make sure your friend eats something.

Every one of us will hit the wall at some point in our life. Showing compassion, not only with others but also with ourselves, is part of being human.

MAXIMIZE SUCCESS

Roz Alford

Roz Alford, the Managing Director at Women Impacting Public Policy, experienced a series of catastrophes in her life that would have overwhelmed the best of us. Her beloved husband was diagnosed with lung cancer and she was diagnosed with breast cancer while he was still in treatment. Then he died suddenly when they were on a cruise together in South America. It was an incredibly challenging process to get him home and there was more trouble waiting for her when she got home:

Even though our business was doing well, I was having issues with my business partner, and I just couldn't handle it anymore. I said, "This is it: I can't have the negativity anymore. I feel like I have a cloud over me. I have got to stop it somehow." I had been trying to buy her out, and she refused. I told her, "Make me an offer. I want out." My husband had wanted me to retire a long time before that and I didn't. It was like, "Okay, it's my time now."

I cut a deal and I didn't have to stay in the business and work for three to five years. It was like the load had totally lifted from me. Did I have the sadness of losing a husband and losing a business? I did. I still feel it, obviously, but what I gained was so much more.

I decided that life was more important than money. Life was more important than having a successful business. It was about family, number one. It was about taking care of me and doing what I wanted for me. My whole goal was finding a way to give back. I sought out organizations that I could work with to help the next generation of women and became very active in women's organizations, first in Partnership Against Domestic Violence then as the foundation chair for the WPO. Then a friend brought me onboard to Women Impacting Public Policy, a nonpartisan group that helps women in multiple organizations be heard in government policy making.

I used to think my business would be my legacy. Sure, I had a great company and I did a lot, but the legacy has to be me and what I give back.

In making the decision to redirect her life in the next meaningful way, Roz reclaimed it all.

How do we conquer catastrophe? With patience, for others as well as ourselves; with actions, small and large; by asking for what we need; and sometimes, as Roz Alford's story illustrates, by shedding what no longer serves us to make room for something new.

For bonus information, practices, and resources:
www.ChasingPerfection.net/book/chapter-4

CHAPTER FIVE

INTUITION IS YOUR SUPERPOWER

Intuition is the intelligence of the heart and the knowledge of the soul. It knows instantly and constantly what can take decades of experience for the mind to logically sort out and understand. Trust it and the reason will follow in time.

—Doe Zantamata, author, artist, and photographer

Your intuition knows what to do. The trick is getting your mind to shut up so you can hear.

—Louise Smith, female NASCAR racer,
dubbed First Lady of Racing

Several years ago, I participated in a women's leadership program focused on embracing what power was in all senses of the word. Intuition wasn't one of the topics listed on the agenda. However, it was an incredible component of our leadership work together. On Friday night, the twenty-six of us were given an assignment: we were to transform a nursing home facility to have a significant, positive impact for its residents and staff—the next day! We were told to bring everything we needed with us. We couldn't spend any of our own money, but we could get people to donate money, items, or their talents. In addition, we could each bring one partner to double the number of our teammates. We didn't know how important that would be.

So we brainstormed and planned for a few hours; people came up with all kinds of things, from doing the residents' hair to clipping nails and doing manicures, to cleaning hallways and walls and bringing in scented candles to improve the institutional smells. Some brought music; some brought games and crafts to do with the residents; someone even received a large food donation. The plan included personal care, creating ambiance, cooking, cleaning, and other activities.

Sounds simple, right? On the day itself, *we were told we could not speak*. We couldn't talk to anyone to coordinate anything when we arrived; we had our plan and had to trust it. The good news was our guests could speak. However, none of them were in on the planning. When you invited your guest, you couldn't explain exactly what that person was going to be doing. You could only explain when and where to meet you.

Surprisingly, this was the most flawlessly executed event I'd ever participated in: Nobody overthought, nobody overstressed. I was moved to tears many times that day by the graceful experience that unfolded. It was beautiful. Afterward, we had a debriefing in which we all talked about the experience. As I recall, it was like being the wind. We were a force. An effortless grace swept through that day through all of us. I knew exactly what to do. I knew exactly where to be. I wasn't worried about anything. I wasn't influenced by anyone's stress, because there wasn't any. There was simply surrender on our parts. We had everything we needed. We let our guests work with the residents and nurses and organize what needed to happen. We could serve and lead from a very graceful place. Service and intuition at work—can you imagine our workplaces collaborating this way? I can.

This is a great illustration of how people work when they are aligned with a common purpose. It reminded me of watching my mom and her sisters in the kitchen preparing a meal together. Although they were all bossy people who knew their way around a kitchen, surprisingly, there were no clashes. There was a grace and ease to their work; everyone knew what to do and how to work with the others, without talking much. When we are quiet, observant, and present, we can access all we need and find our way into that flow. It's the way we connect at an unspoken level, a tether keeping us in sync without effort, intuitive.

Intuition is recognizing a need and filling it easily without effort or stress, offering your unique contribution with nothing more for you to do. It's *knowing* the answer so deeply you do not need data to validate your actions. You don't have to know *how* you know; you just know. And we all have this although we aren't always able to access it.

WHAT IS INTUITION?

According to the *Oxford Dictionary* "intuition" is defined as: "the ability to understand something instinctively without the need for conscious reasoning." How important is it? A lot of very intelligent people have weighed in on that. Steve Jobs said, "Intuition is more powerful than intellect," but people give more weight to intellect. Intuition gets a bad rap, often dismissed as New Age mumbo jumbo that has no place in our rational world. What we call intuition or "gut feeling" is the product of a complex interplay between our instincts, and our conscious and unconscious minds. We know without knowing why or how we know, and it's no less valid; the research supports its value. Logical people aren't comfortable listening to their intuitive voice: Malcolm Gladwell references this in his book *Blink*. Logical people spend far more time validating something their gut told them was true from the very beginning than do those of us who trust our intuition.

If you're not in the habit of trusting your intuition or aren't sure you can rely on it, you can connect with your intuitive abilities by learning to listen to your inner voice. The key to reconnection is creating the quiet space in which it can happen, disconnecting and unplugging technology, and allowing intuition to happen in that space.

PRACTICES FOR SUCCESS

How Can You Get In Touch with Your Intuition?

Some people go to a retreat. There are all kinds: some are private, some are associated with various religious faiths, some are silent—no talking allowed. What they usually have in common is their focus on isolating you; this is not a vacation with friends.

Many people find quiet space by participating in yoga or Pilates classes, not the pumped-up versions with music playing but the more Zen-influenced classes in which people are quietly moving their bodies. Beyond meditation, I find that I'm able to get to my quiet place when I'm in the shower. I've mentioned this in my sessions with leadership teams, and 100 percent of those team members agree there's something about warm water cascading over you that frees you up and ideas start to flow. For some people, it's walking in the woods, riding their bike, or listening to music. For others, it's reading. Wherever you find it, I think your quiet place lives right next door to creativity, and great things await where there is intuitive space.

I find hanging out with animals (most often my bulldog) connects me to my intuition. There's something uniquely available when you're with animals. There are no expectations; you can come as you are and be unconditionally loved and accepted in return. Some dear friends own horses and I enjoy visiting their arena. Riding a horse is an incredibly meditative interaction that is conducive to getting in a rhythm and working with the animal. When you get in the rhythm with your horse, suddenly you're connected to another place inside you as well.

WHAT BLOCKS US FROM ACCESSING OUR INTUITION?

Being busy; when we're doing too much, we lose touch with our internal alignment and what our inner wisdom is trying to tell us because your intuitive voice isn't going to shout to get your attention; it's going to whisper. Being in the grip of strong emotion will make us deaf to it as well. For most of us, most days, it's there, even if we don't realize it. Intuition makes you pick up the phone and call friends because they've been on your mind, and, in turn, they tell you they were just about to call you too!

As many people are, I'm often busy, and it's tough to make the time to just "be" in my life: not being overscheduled, not worrying about getting my to-do list done, and not turning on a device to fill the space. It's all about taking the time to sit and dream, wonder, ponder while taking a walk or riding a bike, peer at a lake or enjoy a sunset, drive with the top down and radio off along a quiet road, listening. That's when the magic happens. Clarity, creativity, opportunity; it's all there in that space waiting for you.

IMMEDIATE BENEFITS OF YOUR INTUITION

When you're in touch with your intuition, you're more effective—and you're less stressed. I believe you create your own stress. For example, traffic is not an inherently stressful event; you bring the interpretation of stress to it. Some people react to it with gratitude: "Awesome, more time to listen to my audio book," or "I'm enjoying the person in the car with me and now we have more time together." Some people see it as a business opportunity: "Great, I was able to make seven phone calls." Others scream at the cars, flipping them off and driving erratically. (For the record, I have done all of the above.)

So what's behind the difference in these attitudes? When you're at the intersection where peace meets grace, you're centered enough to ask, "What's the good news about this?" or "How do I make this work for me?" When you're tuned in to it, there's usually a dramatic reduction in stress because when you're "on" with your gut, you're aligned with energy well beyond your intellect. The logical mind is a wonderful tool, but it has its limits. When you're truly aligned—mind, body, spirit, intellect—you're open and receptive to bigger things. That's when you find the love of your life; that's when you find your next big business solution, and you might even find the hobby you always wanted. It's when you suddenly see a way to streamline a bottlenecked process or come up with a brilliant new business offering. That's when you take a risk, take the plunge, dare to do something you'd never thought you would or could. This is when innovation happens.

A client of mine shared a story recently. She and her significant other were in Costa Rica with their grown kids, sitting on a beach and watching them surf. "Everything was so perfect and so peaceful," she told me. "We were in this moment where we looked at each other and said, 'It can't get better than this; we're so grateful to be here.' The next thing I knew, we were in a realtor's office saying, 'We'd like to buy some property.'" And they did! The next day, they purchased, right on the spot, the last lot in a new development. She admitted they'd never before made such an impulsive purchase, let alone a home—yet they both *knew* it was the right thing to do. We had an entire dialogue about how she's at peace with it, no second guessing or buyer's remorse. "It doesn't make sense," she said, "but we both know it was the right thing to do."

MAXIMIZE SUCCESS

Sandy Hansen-Wolff

Sandy Hansen-Wolff counts on her intuition in many ways:

One thing that has served me very well is using my intuitive abilities to work with people. I'm a lifetime learner and over the last five or so years, I've really been focusing on how to embrace what I intuitively know is true about myself and blast that out for my own passions toward my life's purpose.

I've always believed that whatever you can think, you can create. I live by my own notion that the only difference between a huge dream and a reality are the action steps in between. A good definition of the intuitive process that I keep in my mind is force versus flow. Sometimes we try so hard to force things to happen only to see them fall apart. It still takes work and dedication, but there are so many times when, if you're in the flow more than you're forcing, things turn out so beautifully, as though they were meant to go that way in the first place. I think we tend to be more in the force than the flow a lot of the time. If we just take a collective step back, even for five or ten minutes each morning before we start our day, we can make room for the flow to happen."

Sandy believes in good self-care on both the physical and spiritual level and makes time every day for meditation and movement.

TESTING YOUR INTUITION

When I trained coaches for certification, participants did an exercise called the Wilderness Survival Worksheet. On it were twelve questions and three possible answers for each question, such as:

> The day becomes dry and hot. You have a full canteen of water (about one liter) with you, you should …

> You find yourself rim rocked; your only route is up. The
> way is mossy, slippery rock. You should …

Mind you, those doing the exercise were, by and large, not wilderness experts, so these were not familiar situations.

After doing the exercise individually, people were divided into small groups to talk about their answers and decide collectively which answers were correct. If your answer was altered by the discussion, you'd note it on your worksheet, and then we shared the answers with the entire group. It was fascinating because the individual scores went *down* when people worked in a group. Why? When people dispersed into groups, two things happened: everyone deferred to the person who *seemed* the most knowledgeable or the most experienced because they were most persuasive. They didn't have to be the loudest or the bossiest but simply the ones who were the surest of themselves. We would watch it happen in every group: people would give their answers, and when someone else challenged them, if they didn't have a good enough logical bargaining chip—if they admitted, for instance, that their answer just "felt right"—they were immediately dismissed. There was some vindication of the intuitive people when the worksheets were scored, as they'd often done better than those who'd been so sure of themselves logically. Given that some of these questions concern life or death situations, it's evident that groupthink wasn't always the best way to reach those decisions. Our tendency is to rely on facts when intuition is actually our superpower. Knowing how to harness the power of intuition is our competitive advantage at work and home.

YOUR BRAIN WILL TRY TO STOP YOU

Your brain's most important job is to protect your body, to minimize risk, and to maintain life as it is. When we find ourselves in a corner, we're going to instinctively rely on logic or past experience. Often, logic fails us, and what worked in the past doesn't always work in a new, similar situation. Letting go of the past and being open to questioning what's possible unlocks the door to your inner wisdom.

Grace is there to be found, if you can quiet your mental chatter and plug into it, through practices such as meditation, journaling, and being in nature. Intuition is heard when you crack the door open to let what's gnawing at you into your conscious awareness. Some people are more skilled at letting it in. The rest of us can quiet ourselves for temporary periods and access it. The more you practice quieting your mind, the more freely your intuition will flow.

PRACTICES FOR SUCCESS

Establishing a Daily Meditation from Jack Kornfield

Instruction for Meditation

Please do this exercise for ten to twenty minutes each day. You can meditate wherever you can sit easily with minimal disturbance: a corner of your bedroom or any other quiet spot in your home. Use either a meditation cushion or chair. Arrange what is around so that you are reminded of your meditative purpose, so that it feels like a sacred and peaceful space.

Select a regular time for practice that suits your schedule and temperament. If you are a morning person, experiment with a sitting before breakfast. If evening fits your temperament or schedule better, try that first. Begin with sitting ten or twenty minutes at a time. Later you can sit longer or more frequently. Daily meditation can become like bathing or tooth brushing. It can bring a regular cleansing and calming to your heart and mind.

Find a posture on a chair or cushion in which you can easily sit erect without being rigid. Let your body be firmly planted on the earth, your hands resting easily, your heart soft, your eyes closed gently. At first feel your body and consciously soften any obvious tension. Let go of any habitual thoughts or plans. Bring your attention to feel the sensations of your breathing. Take a few deep breaths to sense where you can feel the breath most easily, as coolness or tingling in the nostrils or throat, as movement of the chest, or as rise and fall of the belly. Then let your breath be natural. Feel the sensations of your natural breathing very carefully, relaxing into each breath as you feel it, noticing how the soft sensations of breathing come and go with the changing breath.

After a few breaths your mind will probably wander. When you notice this, no matter how long or short a time you have been away, simply come back to the next breath. Before you return, you can mindfully acknowledge where you have gone with a soft word in the back of your mind, such as "thinking," "wandering," "hearing," "itching." After softly and silently naming to yourself where your attention has been, gently and directly return to feel the next breath. Later on in your meditation, you will be able to work with the places your mind wanders to, but for the initial training, one word of acknowledgement and a simple return to the breath is best.

As you sit, let the breath change rhythms naturally, allowing it to be short, long, fast, slow, rough, or easy. Calm yourself by relaxing into the breath. When your breath becomes soft, let your attention become gentle and careful, as soft as the breath itself.

Like training a puppy, gently bring yourself back a thousand times. Over the weeks and months of this practice you will gradually learn to calm and center yourself using the breath. There will be many cycles in this process; stormy days alternating with clear days. Just stay with it. As you do, listening deeply, you will find the breath helping to connect and quiet your whole body and mind.

After developing some calm skills, and connecting with your breath, you can then extend your range of meditation to include healing and awareness of all levels of your body and mind. You will discover how awareness of your breath can serve as a steady basis for all you do.

Laurie Wondra is someone who trusts her intuition. I met her years ago when I was briefly in IT recruiting. She was a reference check for a candidate my team was trying to place. I didn't know her from Adam. We had a nice initial phone conversation, and at the end of the phone call, we decided we would get together for coffee. Now that was a strange thing to happen as a result of a reference check, yet the connection was strong and made sense to us both, intuitively. So we had coffee together and by the end of our conversation, she had learned I was a trainer and coach who taught and certified coaches, among other things.

She said, "I'd like to hire you as my coach." I said, "That's great, but I'm at capacity. I have this full-time job in IT recruiting. I just left my business partnership, and I'm trying to keep things simple." I liked her and I wanted to work with her, but I hesitated to take on a client because I didn't think I had the time.

But she persisted: "No, I really want to hire you. What would it cost?" I realized she was intent on closing the deal, and she wasn't going to take no for an answer. I figured, *Fine—I'm going to charge a fee that's so high she has to say no to me then*. I said, "I charge $200 an hour," which in 1998 seemed like a lot of money and definitely more than I had ever been comfortable asking for up to that point in my life. She didn't hesitate: "Awesome! When can we start?"

I remember I left that lunch wondering what had just happened there. I had been sure she would say no, and now she was a client and I was excited to have her. How had that happened?

What I didn't know then was that from a very young age, Laurie had known she was psychic.

MAXIMIZE SUCCESS

Laurie Wondra

Laurie Wondra's bio seems like an exercise in incongruity: She has spent her career as an executive in the global IT field but is also the owner of, and shaman at, YourLifeCore. At the heart of her work is her superbly developed intuition and a deep spirituality that's been integral to her life since childhood.

Laurie's gifts are useful in the workplace because she can intuitively see what is below the surface. In tense meetings Laurie will watch the energy and auras of those around her and be able to "tell that there's something simmering even though they might look very normal to the other people around the table. Sometimes it's uncomfortable because there is outright tension, or there is something I pick up about somebody that they're not saying." Laurie's training with me in coaching and communication has helped her handle these situations with grace; she has the skills to "draw those things out without making people feel like they're put on the spot or embarrassing them." The intuition Laurie speaks of is part of what makes people uncomfortable about the metaphysical. "It's scary for people who might think you know things about them," explains Laurie. Another piece of the intuition, however, is knowing when to let things just be; Laurie does this also.

"Everybody has the same ability if they want to evolve and develop it," Laurie says. She makes the analogy that developing metaphysical abilities is similar to noticing the air conditioner turning on. "It's just a subtle shift in the breeze, similar to life. There are little, subtle things that, unless you pay attention, pass right by you. But if you pay attention to the signals, they're around you all the time." Spending time in nature, yoga, journaling, and music can all help develop metaphysical gifts. Laurie advises meditation as well but also shares a modification beginners will appreciate: "If you have a busy mind, another way is string thinking: allow yourself to think wherever your mind wants to go. After a while, you'll get tired of your own thoughts, and then your mind will be clear for the pure thoughts to come in."

She knew very early that she had a spiritual connection most people couldn't understand. Her more conservative parents weren't thrilled and encouraged her to turn away from those interests to science. That's how she ended up with a career in IT, which she says grounded her in another way and gave her mind a balance it might otherwise have lacked. Laurie became a certified coach and we conducted trainings together for more than five years. Our work has evolved with each of us as a client of the other, learning together. When we met and I began coaching her, it was clear we'd connected because she wanted to access that quieted part of herself. I remember her asking me, "How do I get back to that?" My answer was, "You already know the answer to that, but you just don't trust it."

Like Dorothy with her ruby slippers, she realized she'd had the tools to find the way back to where she wanted to go all along—and now she was ready to use them. When we met, she was a powerhouse in the global IT world, and she still is, but she's also a practicing shaman who leads groups of seekers on spiritual pilgrimages to places such as Sedona, Greece, and northern Minnesota, and she teaches them to get in touch with their spiritual selves and the intuitive side that life can stifle. More and more often, these seekers include CEOs and other business leaders looking to boost their intuition and performance. When my mother passed, Laurie was the person who delivered messages to me that only my mom could have sent, things Laurie couldn't have known about me. Even as I heard them, it was impossible for me to totally divorce myself from skepticism—but believe me, they resonated, and they still do.

Spirituality isn't something most of us are willing to openly talk about, particularly if it's an alternative kind that doesn't fit neatly into traditional models. I can talk about it with you if you're a friend of mine, but it's probably not something I'd bring up at a cocktail party or networking event. Finding your spiritual center and honoring it is critical. Too often we quiet that voice, when we could be asking, "What makes me feel grounded and connected? What's the right choice for me? What brings me joy? What *feels* right for me?"

Most of us are overwhelmed by the sheer volume (in both senses of the word) of information that comes at us all day. I hear from more and more people that they can't handle social media anymore because there's just too much of it. Maybe that's your intuition taking over: "This isn't working for me. It's causing a disruption to my peace and connectedness and it's negatively impacting my thinking and creativity. It's directly affecting how I'm being in the world." Pulling back from technology, doing things the old-school way is good for the soul.

You need to find your healthy balance between your spiritual, intuitive self and your logical mind. They don't negate each other; they enhance and support each other. Using practices to open your mind to your subtle, quiet voice may be how you accelerate your next great breakthrough, whether that's seeing a new path for yourself or for your business, or recognizing the love of your life when that person shows up. It may be subtle right now, but intuition is your superpower.

For bonus information, practices, and resources:
www.ChasingPerfection.net/book/chapter-5

CHAPTER SIX

GAME CHANGERS AND TRAILBLAZERS

If you truly want to improve your self-worth,
stop giving other people the calculator.

—Tim Fargo, author and entrepreneur

The question isn't who's going to let me;
it's who's going to stop me?

—Ayn Rand, philosopher and author

Trailblazing is tough work; ask any woman in the workforce, whether she's a CEO or an executive assistant. You can't be all things to all people, though everything you've been taught will tell you that you're supposed to try. Inevitably, there are trade-offs, and people will tell you that you shouldn't, you can't, and you're going against the grain. The trick is to find an equal amount of support and positive people who will tell you to keep doing what you're doing because it matters.

For every woman who has succeeded, there's a host of women preceding her who did something courageous, something nonconformist that was probably not received well at the time, but they dared to interrupt the status quo. Emma Watson's speech about feminism hits the nail on the head: "It isn't against anyone. It's for everyone. It's about equalizing things. How can we effect change when only half of the world is invited to the table?" It's such a thoughtful, compelling, and profound question. In order to create understanding, you've got to have the healthy conflict that goes along with forging new turf, and that's what feminism is about. We still have a long way to go to reach equality, but I only have to look at my mother's life to realize how far we've come in a generation.

My mom was a devout Catholic, educated in parochial school when it was still the old-school, hardcore, rulers-to-the-back-of-the-hand kind of system. When she was a teenager, she fell in love with my dad who was a Protestant. At that time, a Protestant-Catholic marriage was called a mixed marriage and it was a very big deal. When they first fell in love, she was only sixteen, and he was twenty-two and about to go into the service. Within two years, he was honorably discharged, and they wanted to get married, but her parents absolutely forbade it, so they eloped. My mom became pregnant right away. Her family was not happy and shunned my parents because they hadn't been "properly" married in the Catholic Church. Mind you, my parents met at my uncle and aunt's wedding (my dad's sister married my mom's brother). So my uncle married a non-Catholic girl, but that was all right because the expectation was that, as the wife, she would give up her faith and take up her husband's, which she did. They were not shunned, only my parents. Talk about hypocrisy!

Somehow, through all this, my mother held on to her faith and her religion; she never stopped going to church, even though my father didn't go with her. Her first pregnancy was a difficult one, and she nearly died giving birth to my oldest brother. Afterward, her doctor told her that if she were to have another child, it could kill her, and she needed to use birth control. Well, that flew in the face of everything the Catholic Church taught at that time; birth control was not allowed. If you were meant to have children, you'd have them, period. Now she was facing a moral dilemma: Should she protect her own life, take birth control, and fall away from the Catholic Church, or should she continue going to church and rolling the dice, and if it were God's will, let another childbirth kill her? Ultimately, she decided to use birth control, and although she raised her children to be Catholics, she went to church less frequently. She had two more sons, without problems, thankfully. Then, twelve years later, she had me.

PRACTICES FOR SUCCESS

Stop Apologizing

Too many of the women I work with are battling guilt, and they spend much too much time apologizing for what they're doing and things they haven't done perfectly. I help them to understand the difference between saying, "I'm sorry," which implies that they've done something wrong, and "I apologize," which suggests that they regret their actions are affecting someone in a less-than-favorable way but doesn't imply they're wrong. Much of the time we're apologizing for being bold and direct, which some people find disruptive— but it's not anything to apologize for. Women are guilty of apologizing when it's unnecessary. Stop it! Disruptive women get things done and make history. We need them.

It sounds like a conventional life in today's terms, but my mom was a rule breaker. She was someone who had eloped, defying her family and religion and choosing her own path. She did what her heart, intuition, and conscience told her was right. She witnessed the 1960s with their upheavals of bra burning and social change, when people started doing what they believed was right, even if it went against the norm. My parents consistently told me, "You can do anything you want to do. We support you, and we love you." My gender had nothing to do with my possibilities. My dad saw things the same way, and up to a point, I was raised with a kind of gender parity that was unusual even then. Dad expected me to mow the lawn and do yard work, and I learned how to fix my car and bait a hook. I also learned from a pro how to iron and cook and clean. I wanted to get a job as early as possible when I was young, and working hard was something we knew well in our family. My parents' philosophy was: "Keep working hard and being smart. You can be the first one in our family to go to college. We'll help you if we can." The self-reliance they encouraged in me really set the stage for who I am and what I believe is possible because, even as they had their gender-specific roles, neither parent put limitations on me.

MAXIMIZE SUCCESS

Marsha Firestone

Most women I work with have stories to tell about their challenges with inequality. Dr. Marsha Firestone is the founder and president of the WPO, begun in 1997 as a peer advisory organization for women who own multimillion-dollar businesses. Marsha earned a doctorate in communication from Columbia University, specializing in the dynamics of small groups. This was at a time when there was more opposition to women in the workplace. The day she defended her dissertation, there was palpable hostility in the room. The all-male review committee facing her made it crystal clear that as far as they were concerned, she had no business being there, and their questions were pointedly con-frontational. As Marsha defended her thesis, the revered social anthropologist Margaret Mead, then a professor at Columbia, entered the room. As Marsha recalls, "When asked for input, Mead turned to the committee and said, 'I think this is the best-written dissertation I've heard in many years. I think it's one of the most profound and necessary skills our world needs around communication and body language.'" Marsha remembered, "It was absolutely a breeze from there forward. Had Margaret Mead not walked in, I might not have gotten my PhD."

Women helping women in the business world is more common now than it used to be, and Marsha was ahead of her time in championing women business owners when she formed the WPO over twenty years ago. "I remember trying to set the amount of money that the women had to generate to qualify for this group, and I remember thinking, *Oh my God, a million dollars is so much*"—and twenty years ago, it was. Her husband gave her the money to pay her first employee, Linda Strapazon, because she had no revenue at the start of this nonprofit. She gathered together a group of women, she started the chapter, and she facilitated one group before deciding she wasn't a great facilitator. At that point, she brought aboard Mindy Goodfriend and Ellie Gordon as facilitators, and she set off to start her next chapter in Los Angeles. All three women are still involved in the organization, and now, twenty years later, it has gone global with over two thousand members.

I've been a WPO chapter chair for over fifteen years and have founded six chapters, five in Minnesota. I've learned so much from these amazing women, all because Marsha determined a need for "a peer advisory group where we can gather women from these businesses that are very much under the radar" since businesswomen weren't publicly touting themselves. Overall, women don't toot their horn very well. (At the first WPO conference, about forty women attended. In 2017 we saw more than 850.)

Marsha told me about an early mentor who consoled her after a setback by telling her she wasn't failing; she just needed to quit for the moment and then move ahead. That's very much the mind-set we need to keep in front of us: as long as we're breathing, the work isn't done. Though you're collecting many supporters along the way, you're also changing a social norm, which is not the same as changing a tire. It's not a simple strategic initiative or a one-time event. You're working to change the way people think, and how social behavior is organized, and support is key. You must gather an army of people who believe as you do, and be able to deafen yourself to those who will tell you it will never work and wonder what you could possibly have been thinking.

PRACTICES FOR SUCCESS

Lose the Naysayers

Do you define what's possible for you and your life, or are your possibilities constrained by what others tell you can or can't be done? Tell the truth. We've all got those people in our lives, the ones who start shaking their heads before we've finished describing a new idea or an opportunity in full. Those are the naysayers, and until you get them out of your life (or at least out of your head), their disempowering messages will undermine your potential.

THE GIFT OF MENTORSHIP

One thing we can do for each other that makes a tremendous difference is to mentor and advocate for other women. I wrote about Rhoda Olsen in chapter 4. We met in 2008 when I was at an incredibly low point in my life. As it happened, I was recruiting members for the WPO, and, within a three-week period, several friends mentioned her as someone I should meet. Her business hadn't hit the billion-dollar mark yet, but she was well on her way. A friend connected us and we had breakfast together.

We bonded quickly and I discovered she was already in a peer learning group, one consisting of men and women. I initially assumed she was a "no" for the WPO, but when she asked me if she could be in both groups, I was thrilled to say yes! By the end of our breakfast we'd had an incredible meeting. I had four pages of notes and was thinking, "Wow!"—and she said, "I'd like to have breakfast again. Would you?"

I remember thinking, "Wow, she wants to have breakfast again with *me*?" and I said, "Absolutely." We met a few more times, and by the third meeting, I had gathered up my courage to ask, "I know you're crazy busy, but would you consider mentoring me?"

She said, "You know what, Sue?"—and I could hear the "no" coming—"I can't do that. The only way it will work is if we mentor one another. You see, I learn as much from you as you learn from me."

I remember feeling dumbstruck. "You've got to be kidding," I said. It was the classiest, most gracious response I'd heard. She was clearly someone who did not need me in her life. "I would be honored as long as you have time," I said.

She told me, "Let's have breakfast every month. I learn a lot from our meetings and I really enjoy spending time with you. We have a lot in common, and you ask great questions." I left the meeting on a cloud. I remember thinking how much better this world would be if people were always this generous with each other. We need to lift each other up, not only blazing the trail but also helping the next generation of leaders to navigate it.

THE NEXT GENERATION IS READY— WILL WE HELP THEM?

My daughter Alexandra is in her twenties. She tells me it feels next to impossible for her to ask someone she admires to have lunch or coffee with her so she can ask for insights or advice. As she puts it, "I just feel lucky to be in the room. Who am I to take up someone's time? I'm the lowest person on the totem pole. I'm just happy to shake somebody's hand. So in terms of asking, 'Hey, can I meet with you?' or 'Would you share insight with me about your industry?'— that's beyond anything I feel comfortable doing because I think, *Here are these people who have fifty million things to do that are way more important than me, and I'm not giving anything back. It's not fair to ask them for something when I'm providing zero.*" Her experience is similar to mine with Rhoda. I remind her she may not be able to offer business insights, but she is letting people talk about who they are, what matters to them, what they love doing, or how they started in business, and this is a gift for them.

Though Alexandra may not deal with the challenges my mom or I did, she tells me she's unsure about having her own kids, because she's not sure she could be the mom she'd want to be while having a great career. That hasn't changed—and it needs to because men aren't torn about choosing between family and a career. We've still got work to do.

PRACTICES FOR SUCCESS

Mentoring

From my experience, mentorship is a gift to both people involved. Are you willing to invest your time and energy sharing what you've learned with the next generation of leaders? If you're starting out, be brave and ask someone whom you admire and with whom you have a rapport to lunch or coffee, and explore the idea of mentorship. Peer groups are another powerful way to connect, educate, and be educated. Seek out groups of professionals in your field or others running businesses. Meet regularly to discuss common issues and exchange business or personal advice and insights. When we help others, we help ourselves. Check the website link at the end of the chapter for a list of peer groups.

BEING HEARD

As women, we often have to push to be heard or acknowledged for our input, particularly in groups where we're outnumbered by men. On multiple occasions, I've offered a useful idea or suggestion to men in my group and *they don't hear me*—and I'm no wallflower. Within a few minutes, one of several things often happens to my suggestion:

it is attributed to another male, suggested as his own idea, or the idea is hijacked and brainstormed as if it had originated with the hijacker.

This happened with a blog post I was asked to write based on some wisdom I shared in a group of over 150 people, mostly male. The leaders of the event approached me to write a blog post about it, which I did. Two weeks after my blog was published to over thirty-five thousand subscribers, another attendee posted his own blog article with the exact same title, quoting me directly with no attribution whatsoever. I reached out to him and suggested he read the original blog including the link and save face by referencing it.

His response via text was that I had simply beaten him to posting the article. He insisted I had stolen the wisdom from another man in the group. I explained it was my wisdom and ended up arguing with him, while he blamed me for not announcing my name prior to communicating with the group. Otherwise, he said, he would've attributed it correctly in his notes. We ended up in a heated phone conversation and he eventually apologized. We'd wasted an hour of time while he blamed me for something that I hadn't done and that had resulted in his mistake, when, instead, he could have realized what he'd missed, apologized, and corrected the mistake.

I'm not unique; most women face situations like this every day, and we need to stand firm, not back down, and communicate well through it while not creating adversarial relationships. Our allies are the men and women we run with to blaze trails and change the game. We can't make it a one-time event; we must persist in effecting change.

PRACTICES FOR SUCCESS

Embrace Your Inner B.I.T.C.H.

Leadership requires making some noise and ruffling feathers, which includes being straightforward and direct. Women are referred to as "bossy," a "ball buster," or a "bitch" when they're told they're coming on too strong. This kind of language is used as a way to make us back off, which demonstrates a double standard: a man coming on strongly isn't called an asshole; he's praised.

When I was in my early twenties, I received some good advice from trainers I admired and respected: They warned me I'd be called a "bitch" by people who felt intimidated by me, and it was a word intended to slow me, diminish me, or shut me up. They suggested that anytime I heard the word *bitch*, I reframe it as an acronym for these words: "Boys, I'm taking charge here," and "Beauty in total control of herself." Now, if someone refers to me or anyone else that way, I'm actually tickled. Reworking some of the less productive messages we receive into affirming messages is part of changing the game!

As we women leaders continue to blaze trails, it's important we all lift other people up as we succeed. Mentoring, joining a peer group, and championing others make us all better. The power is in the *we*.

For bonus information, practices, and resources:
www.ChasingPerfection.net/book/chapter-6

CHAPTER SEVEN

BACKWARD AND IN HEELS

*After all, Ginger Rogers did everything Fred Astaire
did. She just did it backward and in high heels.*
—Bob Thaves, creator of the comic strip *Frank and Earnest*

Being realistic is the most common path to mediocrity.
—Will Smith, actor

We women entrepreneurs are a special breed; we have to be. As women competing in what is in many ways still a man's world, we're expected to be able to do more with less and to settle for less than a man would. Yes, things are better than they were for the generations before us—but not dramatically better. For a woman to succeed in business, she has to be like Ginger Rogers, who did everything Fred Astaire did—in addition to dancing backward and in heels—while looking flawless doing it. Men who persevere are praised for their determination; women who persevere are dismissed as pushy. Personally, I take those kinds of comments as compliments, and they are fuel for my commitment. It's not effective to be angry, so what can you do about it?

You can do everything right—and still lose. That's true for women in all spheres, from the political to the personal. So often, women must face additional challenges as they ascend in their careers, checking all the right boxes as they go, proving themselves again and again, only to be denied the outcome, often for no evident reason, apart from gender. That's why women leaders must be willing to go the extra mile, deliver beyond expectations, and always work on improving, even when it appears to be a disproportionate effort compared with that of others. We have to face adversity with the words: "This will not define me. I will define it." Being good is not good enough.

PRACTICES FOR SUCCESS

Rituals of the Masters

Excellence demands rigor and self-discipline, no matter who you are or how far you've come, and part of that is self-care (see chapter 3). Tony Robbins starts every day with a ten-minute ritual he calls priming: he begins with a set of advanced yoga breathing exercises; he thinks of three things he's grateful for; and he prays for family, friends, and clients. Olympic swimmer Michael Phelps went into every competition with a series of rituals: full-body stretches and warm-up laps as he visualized himself winning and finally pumping himself up with twenty minutes of high-energy music. Sara Criger, president of Mercy Hospital in the Allina Health System, gets up at 4:30 a.m. every day to work out because she's afraid of what will happen if she gets sloppy and lets herself sleep in. Don't let your circumstances limit you; find ways to use them to win. When I'm feeling overwhelmed and pulled in too many directions, I recite a declaration I wrote about myself as a leader, in addition to doing the practices I'm sharing in this book. I think many people miss the mark on the discipline required to live in excellence. They allow themselves to be casual with their practices or they lack consistency. You need to identify the practices that maximize your success and propel you forward and do them consistently. It can't be hit or miss; *your results and your life are the sum of your practices.*

I know many highly successful women whose lives, as seen from outside, look like fairytales, "happily ever after," and a pot of gold at the end of a rainbow. They are women like those highlighted in this book, whose successful business, multiple awards, happy family, and philanthropic work are what most of us see. When you get to know them, you find they are like everyone else. Rhoda Olsen came from an alcoholic, dysfunctional family. Her son has overcome addiction, and she is a cancer survivor. Rhoda remains positive because she believes she's responsible for everything in her life. She'll tell you, "I've got to change my mind. I've got to work on *me*. I've got to figure myself out because I can change whatever is showing up." That's the point of all of this: you must persevere because you'll see whatever you're looking for. If it's bias, you'll find it every time. I'm not talking about denial; it's about finding what you can empower yourself with in a world that may be skewed. Excellence is a matter of continuous self-improvement and leads to success. What if you focused only on who and what moves you forward? How would you change your mind and your motivation? What would you do differently? What would happen with your energy?

Successful entrepreneurs are problem solvers who choose to see possibilities where others see problems. They create solutions, careers, and opportunities, all while making a difference by serving others. Interestingly, the most effective leaders I know are deeply mission driven and never stop raising the bar for themselves. Julie Allinson, who built eyebobs, the eyeglass company, says it so well, "There is no 'there.'" Everybody says, "Once I get to the weekend, I can relax," or "Once I reach this goal, it's going to be different," or "Once our company reaches that target, it's going to be so much better." Regardless of the specific situation, the formula is the same: Once I _____ it will be _____. For most of us, once our goal is reached, we've already chosen the new goal because that's how our brain works. It's a continuous game of self-improvement because there is no *there*. It's like chasing the horizon. While I was on vacation with Julie, I noticed that she never stopped networking. I think she met everyone on this little island in Belize, looking for opportunities for her business. That's a masterful entrepreneur for you: someone who never shuts off business or opportunities.

Many leaders have admitted to me they don't live for vacations; their vocations fulfill them and are always foremost on their minds. Vacation is a way to recharge, gain clarity, and bring renewed creativity to life, and entrepreneurs channel that directly into their business. Work that is unfulfilling contributes to premature aging. Most of us actualize our purpose through our work. If we're doing it right, would we *need* a vacation? We might enjoy one, but we wouldn't *need* one.

HOW DO YOU CREATE AN ENTREPRENEUR?

We know starting a business from scratch requires optimism, focus, incredible tenacity, and the willingness to do it all—often at home as well as the office. Entrepreneurs also demonstrate toughness, comfort with risk, and attention to detail. It shouldn't come as a surprise to discover many entrepreneurs of both genders come from hardworking, humble beginnings; they are often the children of immigrants, raised in small towns, or farming families. Their families believed in hard work and didn't expect to receive anything without effort. They grew up knowing they had to create what they wanted in life and not expect it. Wondering how entrepreneurial you are? Take our quiz via the website link listed at the end of this chapter.

MAXIMIZE SUCCESS

Mahtab Rezai

All woman entrepreneurs face additional scrutiny in competing with men. Add to that the experiences of being an immigrant and a person of color, and success becomes much more challenging to achieve. Mahtab Rezai, principal and CEO of Crux Collaborative, talked with me about her unique perspective as a woman and a first-generation immigrant from Iran:

> One of the main things that our parents taught us as women was: "You have to be twice as good, twice as prepared, twice as effective to get half the credit." I think recognizing that being mediocre was never an option made me realize I have to be excellent in order to sometimes be categorized as able.

Toni Morrison said, "American means white. Everyone else has to hyphenate." What happens when people are operating from that construct unexamined is that they inadvertently "other" you. They make you "other," whether you're brown, whether you have an unfamiliar name, whether you have a different way of dressing. In many instances, they're doing it with good intentions, but it doesn't change the fact that they're "othering" you. Many white Americans feel that their curiosity about someone's name, about someone's background, about what they're wearing, should be rewarded. They're unwilling to examine what happened in the first place, that they felt okay asking that of someone in that way, in that setting. I feel part of my role is being an ambassador. And once I'm able to forge that friendship and respect, to also bring awareness.

America is the only country where people come in as one nationality and, within two to three generations, identify as primarily American. I identify as American wholeheartedly. I also identify as an immigrant wholeheartedly. To me, these are great things. I identify as a woman. I identify as a person of color. These are not contradictions. America can house all of that—and does. The color of America is changing, but the spirit of it is very much intact.

Championing Others

If you're missing something in your life, the best thing you can do is contribute that very thing. For example, if you're feeling a lack of joy, you create joy for someone else. If you're feeling unappreciated, go out of your way to acknowledge and appreciate others. By doing this, you will generate what you "lack" in abundance. In the same way, if you perceive discrimination, offer acceptance and inclusivity. The only work to do is on ourselves through the lens with which we are experiencing the world. Absolutely everything else is out of our control.

Kids who grow up learning to do for themselves are more likely to be optimistic problem solvers because they become practiced in making things happen. For those who become entrepreneurs, this optimism supports them in starting a business, working to effect change in the world, and seeing possibilities where other people see roadblocks and problems. For those of us who grew up with parents from the Depression era, we were fortunate our parents weren't focused on accumulating material things. They concentrated on doing the right thing and having a good life. They understood we needed to be strong to face the challenges life would offer us. As a sixteen-year-old, I was expected to find and pay for my own health insurance when my dad retired, and I bought and maintained my own car. I heard the words, "You can figure it out," a lot when I was growing up. This grooming made me resourceful and self-reliant; it's also the bedrock for becoming an entrepreneur.

There are infinite ways to handle every set of circumstances, but there aren't always easy answers: How do I find the *best* solution out of many alternatives, not just *any* solution? I think people will often latch on to *one* solution and run with it until it doesn't work, rather than working to find the *best* solution for the existing circumstances. This is not about chasing perfection, however, because "perfect is the enemy of done," as my friend Mike Paton says. This is about delivering excellence, and excellence is a byproduct of mastery which comes from living our practices. *Our lives and experiences are the sum total of our practices at any given time.* Sometimes, it's trial and error; sometimes, it's trial by fire because life doesn't hand you the case study version for living.

EXCELLENCE VERSUS PERFECTION

I believe success is a learning disability. What most people call failure is where learning occurs. We tend to make formulas for our winning strategies, and formulas break down. When that happens, we don't know what to do when our winning strategies fail. We default to our familiar strategies and often drive ourselves to exhaustion by working harder when really it's the strategy that's not working. It's like trying to drive a nail into wood with a screwdriver; it's the wrong tool for the job and it doesn't work. What can you learn by letting go of doing what you've always done? How can you become a more open-minded leader when things aren't working? How can you include others when creating a new solution?

EXCELLENCE

Perfection is being right.
EXCELLENCE is willing to be wrong.

Perfection brings on fear.
EXCELLENCE encourages risk.

Perfection leads to anger and frustration.
EXCELLENCE generates power.

Perfection is being in control.
EXCELLENCE is being spontaneous.

Perfection is judgment.
EXCELLENCE is acceptance.

Perfection is taking.
EXCELLENCE is giving.

Perfection is doubt.
EXCELLENCE is letting it flow.

Perfection is destination.
EXCELLENCE is journey.

EXPERIENCE EXCELLENCE in your life!

MAXIMIZE SUCCESS

Julie Allinson

Julie Allinson's signature style and sense of humor are the cornerstones of eyebobs, an eyeglass company that caters to the "irreverent and slightly jaded," which embodies Julie's approach to life. She and her husband, Paul, founded the company in 2001 and nurtured the business through growth, popularity, and partial sale to private equity investors. No longer CEO, Julie is learning to let go while creating a bigger vision (pun intended).

Julie says the greatest lesson she's learned in business is that "you can do it." Growing up on a small farm in Iowa gave Julie the opportunity to do many things and provided her with a confidence she never questioned, which led to success as an entrepreneur. "There were fifty-two students in my class," Julie remembers. "Hell, why not be on the golf team, basketball team, student council, and honors society? Growing up that way, you don't think those things aren't possible." Julie's mom reinforced this mentality, instilling in Julie a glass-half-full sense of optimism. "Anyone can be an entrepreneur," Julie says, "but I think it is fear that holds people back. You just have to be dumb enough to do it and not know or ignore the possibility that you can fail." This belief in herself, and a need for stylish reading glasses, were the catalyst for Julie to start eyebobs.

I don't expect life to turn out perfectly. I expect things to go well because I'm committed to having them go well, but I don't expect them to go well because that's what the world owes me. In fact, I expect the world to challenge me. I expect there will be curveballs. It's never convenient or necessarily easy, but all of it makes me better. It becomes a puzzle to solve, with the challenges that arise, instead of, "Wow, this is a lot of work," because I don't look at it as work. It's exciting to me to be able to win at things I didn't know how to do previously. The challenge of it is actually where the energy comes from, not the actual outcome; though that is the cherry on top!

PRESSURE IS THE PRICE YOU PAY FOR BEING AT THE TABLE

Leaders must learn to manage pressure, and for women "backward and in heels" is the reality we accept. How you reframe that is what matters. Success is looking at a challenging situation and asking yourself who you need to become to succeed. If it's a compelling enough outcome, who you become in the process of succeeding is the real win. There's no big epiphany at the end; epiphanies happen all along the way. The results are simply the outcome of your commitment. Many people miss the joy along the journey because they believe joy is the end result. We put all our chips in getting there versus being present to what we're learning and who we're becoming while getting there. It was the original "backward-and-in-heels" dance icon herself, Ginger Rogers, who said, "The only way to enjoy anything in this life is to earn it first."

For bonus information, practices, and resources:
www.ChasingPerfection.net/book/chapter-7

CHAPTER EIGHT

POURING GAS ON THE FIRE

If you aren't making a difference in other people's lives,
you shouldn't be in business. It's that simple.

—Sir Richard Branson, English business
magnate and founder of the Virgin Group

If you think you are too small to make a difference, try
spending the night in a closed room with a mosquito.

—African proverb

Philanthropy and entrepreneurship go together, and the majority of business owners I know are deeply invested in giving back in a myriad of ways. The idea that they can make the world better, while bettering themselves in the world, drives them and all they do. Some get their company and their employees involved; some have pet projects here or abroad; others are active on boards. Their passion is so great I've wondered whether their businesses came into being simply to support their philanthropic interests.

Why does the challenge of making the world a better place speak to these passionate leaders? As explained in chapter 7, entre-

preneurs see challenges as opportunities. When they hit a wall, they regroup quickly. Hiding within every problem is a big opportunity for something more spectacular to emerge. And when you're someone who solves problems for a living, your take is: "The world just handed me another chance to help others, so what can I do with this one?" Challenges pour gas on the fire.

In my twenties, I quickly realized that someone telling me I couldn't accomplish whatever I was trying to do would kick me into high gear to make it happen. I found a lot of my motivation came from speaking with well-intentioned, smart people who told me all the reasons why things couldn't happen and why I shouldn't waste my time. I never responded with, "Oh, that makes sense. I should stop." Instead, I'd say something like, "Thanks for your help." Or "Watch me." Leaders with philanthropic drive are wired the same way: they often need a bit of grounded opposition to catalyze their efforts. And although they're all successful people, money isn't the primary thing driving them.

SOMETIMES WE LOSE OUR WAY ...

People get in ruts in their life, often around midlife. They wonder, *Wait. What was it all for?* At some point, they forget they have a choice; they begin to settle for whatever happens. But the fact is you *always* have the option to choose. It's never too late to redesign your life to align with your dreams. Do you live by design or by default? Either way, it's up to you.

When you finish school, you step out into the world as a working adult; you begin to make choices and become encumbered with responsibilities. Before you know it, you can feel boxed in. That's when you can begin to lose sight of your dreams and how you will expand your role in the world. In my work, I often witness people getting a strong wake-up call goading them into action, or they start to decline in life, not because they're "less than" but because they *settle*. They settle for what's available, not what's possible, and accept the predictable path, forgetting they *chose* that path. The only way to change direction is to step back, take a critical look at the life you've created, and decide if it's the one you want or the one you've defaulted to.

CONNECT TO YOUR CAUSE

Deep down, we all want to know we matter. We want to connect on a personal level with what we are here for—and separate that from what we've been told it ought to be or what we've always done, because we're all called to something different. Your purpose doesn't have to be grandiose—for example, ending world hunger. For some people, it's simple: loving their family fully and making it the best it can be. The concept of purpose is different for everyone.

I did a transformational training program in my twenties and I was all fired up about it. When I'm passionate about something, *everyone* around me hears about it. So I sat down with my mother and earnestly suggested she was meant for more than being "just a mom," because she was one of the most capable, loving, powerful people I knew. Well intentioned, yet utterly unaware of how condescending I sounded, I told her she could be so much more and positively impact so many more people by taking training sessions and expanding this nice little life she had. Mom heard what I was saying, but she also heard the judgment in it. I vividly remember her telling me, in a very kind but firm way, "If I do nothing more than raise a great family, with wonderful grandchildren, my work is done." That's exactly what she did, and by raising strong and capable children, her work had a positive ripple effect on the world beyond our home's walls through all of us.

I realized I had some growing up to do. Not everybody's called to be Harriet Tubman, Gandhi, or Susan B. Anthony. Mom was tremendously strong and caring, and her mission was clear. Her passion for her family lives through me because of it.

MAXIMIZE SUCCESS

Kate Grathwol

Kate Grathwol is president/CEO of Vision Loss Resources (VLR), a nonprofit organization and Minnesota's largest provider of services, skills, and support for people who are experiencing vision loss. VLR is partially funded by Contract Production Services (CPS), a quick-turn, multifaceted, outsource packaging assembly, and light manufacturing company that was developed to help VLR express its service and community-oriented values.

Managing the competing needs of a business and a social service agency can be difficult, but Kate balances the two by staying true to the mission and reminding both businesses they feed each other. "We all do better when we all do better," explains Kate. "The most important thing is that our clients are being served and they are happy. It is a juggling act, but the overarching theme is service before self." This service continues to provide inspiration after Kate's many years of serving as CEO. "Many of our clients come through the door terrified because they have lost their vision and therefore their independence," Kate explains. "After we teach them skills and share our resources, they come back to life. They realize there is a way to go on living and completely embrace it."

Much of Kate's leadership philosophy comes from lessons she's learned in life. "We all want the same thing," she believes. "We want food, shelter, and community for ourselves and loved ones. We're at work because we want those things, but we also want to be part of the greater community and to help each other. We're all on the same journey, and we're all here to help each other on that journey." This belief fits perfectly with the relationship between VLR and CPS: 100 percent of CPS profits go to the social services organization.

BE THE CHANGE

Mahatma Gandhi is often incorrectly quoted (which doesn't diminish the relevance of the quote) as saying, "You must be the change you wish to see in the world." Yet it's easy to be sidetracked from what's important and meaningful. At junctures in our lives when we're least confident and most doubtful about our own abilities, we question if our life is working, if what we do and have is really what life's all about. We hit that wall in life and look for something external to change. We might change a relationship, or leave a job, or lose some weight, or cut our hair. We immerse ourselves into whatever distraction holds the most appeal, whether that's shopping, sex, food, work, alcohol, or drugs, because we don't know how to deal with our feelings of discomfort. It takes wisdom and patience to be able to sit with discomfort and not become "busy" to avoid it.

I'm a workaholic, so my solution is always to do more, because I can ignore the discomfort when I'm checking accomplishments off my list. That makes me feel better temporarily, but inside, I'm always uncomfortably aware that what I'm doing isn't fundamentally changing what's not working, I'm just distracting myself from it. When I'm purpose driven, I will observe myself becoming busier, and I can choose to stop. Many people haven't developed the ability to stop and observe themselves. We live in a quick-fix culture where it's wrong to feel bad. Instead of learning how to cope and work through it, we medicate it with our *isms* or worse. We've bought into some ideal that we should always feel good. When life is really challenging, do you have the patience and the wisdom to differentiate personal growth from a Band-Aid? This is where purpose work matters: it helps us to correct our behaviors based on what matters most and returns us to understanding what drives us and what's misaligned at the moment. Purpose work moves us to ask bigger, deeper questions resulting in the bedrock we'll build our life upon.

PRACTICES FOR SUCCESS

Purpose Work

What do you believe is a life worth living? What does that life look like, minus your parents' assumptions, society's assumptions, and your friends' assumptions, along with the influences of the media? The exercise included here will help you get in touch with what matters most to you. It's incredibly powerful; it lets your mind roam and it opens possibilities. Purpose work offers you the opportunity to be a detective in your own life. Your purpose will become evident after you explore your responses to the following questions.

Respond to the following in writing:

1. List the ten most important values in your life—how you really live, not how a "good" person lives.

2. List the five people you admire most and explain why. They can be historical figures, but you need to have intimate information about them.

3. List the three most important events in your life and elaborate on why they are important to you.

4. List the five biggest problems, issues, and concerns in your neighborhood, community, state, or world that you would most *want* to do something about, not what you feel you *should* do something about. Again, explore why these issues are important to you.

5. List five occasions when you felt most at home, or the best fit, or that the best was drawn out of you and explain the basis for choosing these occasions.

Now, review your answers, and ask yourself, "What's one action or practice I could begin today and do daily/weekly/monthly to bring my life into alignment with what's important to me?" Every step carries us forward. You may want to discuss your answers (or do the exercise) with someone close to you and form an accountability partnership with that person.

Having a clear purpose keeps you grounded. You are freer to let things go, such as people, events, and jobs. When you become really clear about your purpose, you let go of everything that isn't "on purpose." You have a foundation from which to say yes and no. The right people become available, opportunities arise, and things show up to catalyze your progress when you function in accordance with your purpose. Your purpose is grounded in bigger things than liking your job, liking your friends, and having the right car. Sure, making a superficial change might give you some immediate pleasure and a moment's peace, but transformation will not occur from the outside in. The real work is waiting to be done from the inside out.

BECOMING PURPOSE-FULL

Nobody can validate your purpose for you. You've got to think things through on your own. There was a period in my life when I'd been let down by my partners, both in business and personally, and I had to do a lot of thinking about what partnership meant because, after all, I was half of that nonworking equation.

I started digging into what partnership meant to me: what I was willing to give, what I expected, what it meant to be a good partner, when I had experienced an excellent partnership and with whom, and what had made it excellent. And I took inventory of the people in my life. I asked myself questions like that for six solid months, in journaling, and while I was walking or biking, and I understood going out and getting my hair cut wouldn't address those concerns for me. I had to align myself with something deeper, irrespective of what other people thought or suggested. I couldn't get the answers I needed outside myself. When you can divorce yourself from needing the approval of others, you will have space to become purposeful.

MAXIMIZE SUCCESS

Amelia Mata

Amelia Mata leads a purpose-driven life. She grew up in the family business, Hennepin Home Health Care (HHHC), a Medicare-certified home health care agency her parents founded in 1974. She's proud of how HHHC helps people continue to live in their homes by providing services such as physical therapy, occupational therapy, nursing, personal care assistants, and home health aide and homemaker services to the elderly, mentally ill, and disabled.

The family business was shaken when her father died at forty-eight years old, and Amelia watched as her mother took charge of HHHC. Losing her father at a young age impressed upon Amelia that life is short, and seeing her mother successfully run and grow the business showed her it was possible to be a CEO and mother. Following her parents' example and paying attention to the angels she believes watch over her, Amelia Mata lives a life dedicated to serving others through her business. Amelia retained her sense of service when she took the reins as owner and CEO of HHHC.

Amelia started her second business, Under the Weather, in 2004. While Amelia and her husband, Mark, were busy raising two young boys, they discovered there were no structured environments where sick children could be brought for care when their parents needed to work. Under the Weather was born as the place to go when children need supervision but are not quite healthy enough to go to school or day care. Having a secure place for parents to bring their sick children has many positive benefits. "Because they can go in to work, parents don't need to use vacation days—or worse: miss being paid," Amelia says. "It also eliminates the strain placed on coworkers when someone has to call in sick, and it prevents germs from being spread."

By 2012 Amelia was helping people live better every day, but she believed she could do more. "I was at a point in my life where I was set," she says. "I asked myself, 'What else is there?'" She received her answer later that year while attending the WPO annual conference in New Orleans. She heard presenter Pavithra Mehta describe success with a pay-what-you-can model, and while Amelia didn't realize it then, things were in motion. "I couldn't sleep that night," she says. "It was as if the angels were just pecking at me to use this model. The ideas started flooding in and I knew it was something I had to do." When she got home, Amelia shared the idea with her husband, asking him to hear her out before he said no. To her surprise, he liked the idea. At the same time, in the background, Amelia's sons had been watching a TV show featuring a New Orleans food truck selling pay-what-you-can tacos. "I felt like, if this isn't a sign, I don't know what is!" Amelia says. The pay-what-you-can model has been implemented at Under the Weather and Amelia hears stories every day from the families they are helping.

Amelia is now launching Sick Wisdom, a nonprofit offering education, resources, and consulting to families dealing with questions about elder care. "We want to be *the* resource for people who don't know what to do in these situations," she says. Sick Wisdom will work with both corporate and individual clients, who will either pay a consulting fee or donate back to Sick Wisdom. The money donated will directly fund additional care for children and seniors through Under the Weather and HHHC. "This part is the give-back for me," Amelia says. "It's a good 'heart feel' and cements the two businesses together."

EVERY GOOD THING HAS A RIPPLE EFFECT

We don't have to be supremely conscious of the bigger implications of the small, consistent, good things we do on purpose. A bumblebee doesn't travel around thinking its purpose in the world is to sustain life and create beauty. It's focused on gathering pollen and nectar to take back to the hive. Yet, in the course of doing exactly that, bees sustain life and have a tremendous impact on the world.

We don't always see the full picture, the people we're impacting or the world we're enhancing, because when we're immersed in doing things that are aligned with our purpose, we don't realize how the sum of our actions is adding up to something truly magnificent. When you align your life and do things "on purpose," whether your circle is twenty people, two hundred people, or twenty thousand people, the cumulative impact is impressive—and that's true for all of us.

PRACTICES FOR SUCCESS

Career and Life Reflections

Answer these questions and discuss with a trusted partner. Then take action based on what you learn.

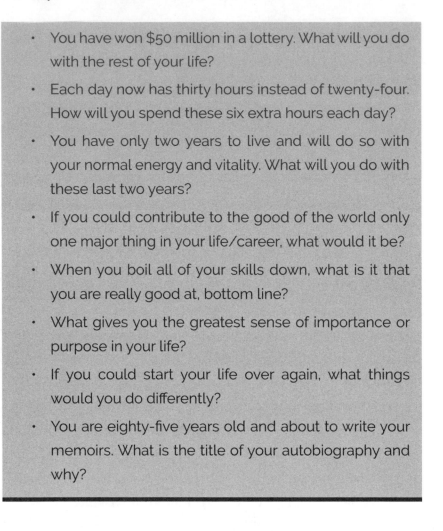

- You have won $50 million in a lottery. What will you do with the rest of your life?

- Each day now has thirty hours instead of twenty-four. How will you spend these six extra hours each day?

- You have only two years to live and will do so with your normal energy and vitality. What will you do with these last two years?

- If you could contribute to the good of the world only one major thing in your life/career, what would it be?

- When you boil all of your skills down, what is it that you are really good at, bottom line?

- What gives you the greatest sense of importance or purpose in your life?

- If you could start your life over again, what things would you do differently?

- You are eighty-five years old and about to write your memoirs. What is the title of your autobiography and why?

We are all driven by a higher purpose. Tapping into it will motivate you in a way little else will. When you stray off track, working through the practices in this chapter will help illuminate what is most meaningful to you. No one else is here to contribute what you are here to contribute. It's time to purposefully maximize your impact and your success.

For bonus information, practices, and resources:
www.ChasingPerfection.net/book/chapter-8

CHAPTER NINE

UNLEARNING TO LEARN

Live as if you were to die tomorrow. Learn
as if you were to live forever.

—Mahatma Gandhi, leader of the Indian independence
movement and antiviolence activist

Knowledge is learning something every day.
Wisdom is letting go of something every day.

—Zen proverb

What's a genuine secret to success, not just reaching it but also sustaining it? You must become a lifelong learner. A common thread I've observed in the lives of successful leaders is a hunger to learn. They're always seeking ways to improve themselves and their performance. They're open to learning in nontraditional ways that fit with their individual aptitudes and learning styles. Just as importantly, they're willing and able to unlearn things that no longer serve them, because without that kind of intellectual house cleaning, there's no new space in which to learn.

Learning can come in many forms, whether it's taking on jobs nobody else wants and mastering them, taking courses on topics unfamiliar to you, podcasts, YouTube, dialogue with others, or creating a reading list intended to expand your mind and interests, to name a few—all of these mechanisms contribute to your insight, your ability to think outside the box and grow in capability. And how you learn best—what kind of "smart" you are—is a completely individualized thing and one it will pay you to understand and explore.

THE DIFFERENT KINDS OF SMART

What kind(s) of smart are you? Howard Gardner, the John H. and Elisabeth A. Hobbs Professor of Cognition and Education at the Harvard Graduate School of Education at Harvard University, has delved deeply into the question of what constitutes intelligence. He believes that IQ tests are a very limited tool for measurement, and humans have multiple kinds of intelligence in differing degrees, depending on the individual. By Thomas Armstrong's definition (Gardner's colleague), intelligence is "the ability to respond successfully to new situations and the capacity to learn from one's past experiences," which means your actions make sense, given the circumstances. It is not necessarily about your IQ level or how well you take tests. If people are imploding around you, do you have the interpersonal and intrapersonal intelligence to navigate difficult conversations? According to Gardner, we've all got abilities in one or more of these intelligences: musical, visual/spatial, linguistic, physical/kinesthetic, logical/mathematical, interpersonal, intrapersonal, naturalistic, and existential—and he's added a possible tenth: pedagogical.

I've helped people assess which of these intelligences they're strongest in and how to learn best with the natural smarts they have.

I know too many adults who'll say things such as, "I'm not a science person," or "I'm terrible at math," or "I don't write well." We all have some limiting beliefs about ourselves because, somewhere along the line, usually in school, we tried something unfamiliar, and we received negative feedback. What most people don't know is *how* they best learn. It's not a question of whether you can learn; if you want to do it, there are ways to get at it differently, and it doesn't have to be hard, and you don't have to suffer while learning.

For example, imagine a young person who is gifted with athletic ability (kinesthetic smart) who tells you he isn't good at math. Imagine offering him a homework assignment to watch three games over the weekend and determine who the best player was, based on yards or points. He'd be learning math through his natural intelligence, which would make it enjoyable and engaging. I believe people can learn more effectively by reframing the information through their unique combination of intelligences. Learning should be fun; it's discovery work. When you're with children, watch them learn; for them, it's exciting and fun, full of expression. When did we lose that enthusiasm? How can we recover it?

PRACTICES FOR SUCCESS

Do Something New

There's tremendous value in putting yourself in the shoes of a beginner. As we grow older, most of us don't learn as many new things as we did when we were kids. In childhood, we're open-minded and willing to experiment, and that's how we learn who we are and what we enjoy. We begin to define—and limit—ourselves by these preferences. At

YESS! we have an exercise called "The 20 Things I Love to Do," which very powerfully demonstrates this. You can find it on our website at the link listed at the end of this chapter.

I'd never have imagined I'd enjoy playing Rock Band on the Wii or going to a monster truck rally—and, to be honest, once was enough for the trucks! I tried them because my son was excited about both, and that was enough to get me to jump in. I'm glad I did. Playing my "fake" drums on Rock Band led me to learn how to play real drums, and though I'm no Neil Peart, I enjoyed learning how to play. Try new vacation spots and new foods. Listen to music you normally don't listen to, or read a book by an author you've never read before. When you start to put up barriers, telling yourself, "I'll never ..." "I can't ..." "It won't ..." "I shouldn't ...," you're limiting yourself to what you already know. Continually practicing having a beginner's mind-set keeps you open and humble while expanding your world. You might find something new you really enjoy, and your brain will stay healthier by building new neuropathways instead of going on autopilot as it does when you're doing what you've always done. Expanding your world, as a beginner exploring new things, keeps you learning.

THE IMPORTANCE OF BEING COACHABLE

When you're struggling to learn something new, hiring a coach may be the shortest route to mastery. Why? For most of us, when we say we're stuck, it's because our thinking is limiting us. We have fixed ideas based on past experiences by which we judge new situations and respond in predictable ways. A coach will help you cut a path through your thicket of preconceptions. As important as it is to have the right coach, being coachable is equally essential.

What does it mean to be coachable? It means being open; it means being in any moment that feels like, looks like, and sounds like moments you've experienced a thousand times before and seeing it with new eyes, listening with new ears, and feeling it in new ways. You have to make space, which means you have to be willing to ask yourself what you *haven't* experienced. Why is being coachable important to learning? If you can't make space to hear and accept contradictions or new information, you can't be coached. If you don't accept the fact that what you already know is a tiny amount of all that's available in the world, no matter how well-informed you are, you're not coachable and will remain right where you are: stuck. Learning only happens when you throw out your fixed assumptions, fixed beliefs, and fixed reality. The biggest barricade to learning can be defined in two words: *I know*. After saying them, *all* learning ceases. For me, the older I get, the less I know. There's much less certainty and much more curiosity. I'm much less likely to assume "that's all there is to know" and more likely to ask what other information may be available and whether I'm willing to be vulnerable and curious to look into it. And I've come to realize that while I may not be the smartest person in the room, I can be the most accessible.

MAXIMIZE SUCCESS

Kay Phillips

Kay Phillips, co-owner and former president of ATEK Companies, is a lifelong learner. She believes learning and leading are closely tied and is "always watching others and seeing how they did something, communicated something, or are thinking about their strategy. I'm constantly watching and taking note of things I want to add to my toolkit or my capabilities." One thing Kay has determined over the years is that different situations require different leadership styles. "There are times you need to be commanding and controlling, but that's rare. I've learned to listen better and be more thoughtful about the team and not just the project."

Kay's biggest leadership lessons have come from "taking on pretty much any crappy job someone would give me." She says this with a laugh. "I learned so many things by doing that, and often took on jobs and did things I didn't have the skill set for. I had to figure things out pretty quickly." Kay admits while she did fail sometimes, the failure *always* resulted in learning.

INFORMATION, KNOWLEDGE, WISDOM, AND LEARNING

Most people confuse knowledge with learning, but they are not the same. Learning equates to behavior in action, really practicing what you consume as information and transform into behavior. Information is different from knowledge and wisdom. *Information* is about reading and retaining some small, specific piece of data online today but having no deeper understanding of it than what was shared online. *Knowledge* is the result of reading something on the Internet, doing further research on it, and discussing it with friends who share what they know as well, so what is now known has more depth. Finally, there's *wisdom*, which I define as knowledge in action, meaning that I've learned the facts, explored the topic in depth *over time*, and practiced using it until it's embodied in me. I can now access all I know without much conscious effort *and* I remain curious and open-minded enough to continue to learn. I can use all I know and flex to the given situation. Over time, this wisdom equates to mastery. I have the experience and confidence of a master, coupled with the willingness and hunger of a beginner. Mastery begins when we approach familiar challenges with new questions, an open heart, and an open mind.

PRACTICES FOR SUCCESS

Peer Learning

Surrounding yourself with people who are smarter than you is a great way to learn. In my experience, leaders learn best from trusted peers with experience because they are challenge-oriented problem solvers. Case studies just aren't as intriguing as being in an experiential setting, a roundtable, or a professional development session where you surround yourself with others from whose experience you benefit. You learn more broadly by questioning how your peers thought through a certain problem, how they approached that problem differently from the way you would approach it, and what questions they asked. My passion for peer learning is based on my own fifteen-plus years of involvement with the WPO, which has provided me with knowledge I couldn't have gained anywhere else.

MAXIMIZE SUCCESS

Lisa David

As a partner of the analytics technology solution firm eCapital Advisors, Lisa David sees learning as an integral part of what she does. Driven by both her intense desire to learn and the care she has for her clients, Lisa is "fascinated by how improving the data agility of a company can improve overall operations and effectiveness." In line with her business background, what fuels Lisa is "really getting to see, meet, and understand all of these different companies while learning what drives them as a business and how they are measured. Every day, I meet with people and realize they care about X because they're in this industry. So my business background is extremely beneficial to my leadership position in technology."

Not only does Lisa need to be a top-tier consultant but she also needs to be an expert in technology services. Because the industry changes so quickly, Lisa says she often does not present the same services from one quarter to the next. "I thrive on learning something new. It's a huge part of me. In this industry, it has to be."

NEW PRACTICES

When you add new practices into your life, ask yourself what you will need to let go of. I can't tell you the last time I regularly watched TV, not because it isn't enjoyable but because I simply have other priorities that serve me better. So I made that choice. Does it mean I never watch TV? No, because if I make it a hard rule to never watch TV, I'm going to miss opportunities such as watching a goofy movie with my kids over the holidays. I make choices to stop doing things in order to make space for what I choose to do. Having a to-do list is great, but what's better is to create a "stop-doing" list as well. When you add something to your to-do list, you must add something to your stop-doing list. Try it. You will choose more wisely!

LEARN TO UNLEARN

As I've said, unlearning is critical to learning because dropping old practices and stale thinking can free up space to learn more effective thinking and behavior. For most of us, our unlearning has to do with what we learned as we were growing up, which no longer serves us, including the "shoulds" we internalized about our roles and responsibilities. We absorbed those expectations, not as choices we made but as byproducts of our families, social norms, education, history, and background. Many of them don't support us in being the best we can be. We may have forgotten we chose them. We accepted what we "should" do and we shoulder those expectations because our environment supports them.

When I became a mom, I had a lot of "shoulds." For instance, I "should" stay in an abusive marriage for my son's sake because I didn't want a broken home. I hoped my husband would change his behavior, and I believed I was strong enough to make those changes happen for all of us. My mother had warned me the day before my wedding that our marriage wasn't going to last; he was not the right person for me. Six years later, I was on my parents' doorstep with my son and a lot to unlearn. I knew I had internal work to do, and I went at it with a vengeance. I started working with a therapist. I went through a twelve-week program at the Domestic Abuse Project. And shortly thereafter, I became a single parent.

Another example comes from later in my life: dating. When I was in my forties and dipping my toe back in the water, I had a lot of rules about meeting people, which I'd carried forward from my twenties. At this point I had income well beyond my college years and a very different life, yet I had a lot of old rules and ideas about dating to unlearn. They were rules that no longer worked for me. It took me five years of dating to unlearn what I thought I knew about myself in terms of relationships and make space for a new approach that I could develop with a true partner.

When I met my husband Kevin, I was crystal clear about what partnership meant to me. He is everything I imagined and beyond: he's kind, smart, handsome, loving, easy to be with, and super competent. We've had similar life experiences, and we are both codependent in our own beautiful way, but we enjoy it because at least we're taking care of each other now! We unlearned what we needed to: those behaviors and patterns that hadn't served us in the past. My self-exploration and redesigned practices over the years paid off, and our partnership is defined by our shared purpose and profound love for each other, which led us to marriage.

PRACTICES FOR SUCCESS

Gaining Time

Do you want more time for the things that matter? Outsource those things that do not bring you joy but which have to get done nevertheless (see the Delegate and Elevate™ exercise in chapter 2). Then let go of any negative preconception you may have about delegating. In my case, both my husband and I enjoy our careers so much that they leave us little time to take care of many tasks involved in home ownership. We've made the choice to use a meal delivery service and to hire a house cleaner, and whatever guilt that might have stirred up in me was alleviated by recognizing we're supporting other small businesses and families by focusing on our quality of life. I've had to reconcile my idea of what I can reasonably expect of myself and let go. By doing so, I have more time to spend with my family, which is worth more than the cash it costs me to hire others.

Winning in the world means being a really good problem solver, because life is made up of a series of circumstances. The quality of your life is determined by how you handle these circumstances at work and at home. As Becky Roloff says, you choose your best set of problems and reframe your thinking to see them as opportunities. When you can do that, you have succeeded because now, whatever happens, you're responding, proactive, and thoughtful. And that's the unlearning and the learning coupled together: "Here we go, a new challenge. I might scrape my knees but it won't be a broken leg. And no matter what, I will be better for it."

Entrepreneurial Operating System® (EOS®): Helping Leadership Teams Learn Together

As a Certified EOS Implementer™, I help people get what they want from their business. I do that by helping them to implement this complete, proven system with simple, practical tools to facilitate three things we call vision, traction, healthy.

1. Vision: First, get your leaders 100 percent on the same page with where your organization is going and how it is going to get there.

2. Traction: Then help your leaders to become more disciplined and accountable, performing really well to achieve every part of your vision.

3. Healthy: Help your leaders to become a healthy, functional, cohesive leadership team because, unfortunately, leaders often don't function well as a team.

From there, as goes your leadership team, so goes the rest of your organization. You get to the point where your entire organization is crystal clear about your vision; everyone involved is much more disciplined and accountable, performing well, gaining consistent traction, and advancing as a healthy, functional, cohesive team.

If any of that resonates with you, we'd love to *give* you ninety minutes of our time to show you how to experience vision, traction, and health in your business with your leadership team. Simply contact us at **info@sayyess.com** and we'll get it scheduled.

Learning new things, learning *how* you learn best, and unlearning things that no longer serve you are all part of being a lifelong learner. The more conscientiously you approach this, the more open and accessible you will be to new ideas, opportunities, and designing the life you want to live at work and home. Your success is equal to your ability to learn what you need to. Maximize it!

For bonus information, practices, and resources:
www.ChasingPerfection.net/book/chapter-9

CHAPTER TEN

ENTITLED TO ENLIGHTENED

Written with Alexandra Stieglbauer

People need to be reminded more than instructed.
—Samuel Johnson, English author and lexicographer

One generation plants the tree; another gets the shade.
—Chinese proverb

We know we can't go anywhere without hearing about the challenges of working with and mentoring younger generations. For our incoming millennial leaders and younger generations, this chapter is also for you and those you work with. From my lens on the world, I believe it all comes down to communication. No matter the generation, if we can communicate more effectively, we can better understand those around us. Please note I'm a communication expert, not a generational guru. I believe the research on generations in the workplace is real and informative. I challenge the belief that any generation (spanning twenty years) can be categorized and generalized in behavior.

Millennials are the most written-about generation in history. Their communication and worldview is different from that of preceding generations, thanks, in part, to technology. I feel a responsibility to extend a hand to the incoming generations of leaders because I'm acutely aware we all stand on the shoulders of those who came before us. With the advent of smartphones, millennials were the first generation to have 24/7 access to answers and each other. Their phones are an extension of themselves. The incoming Generation Edge (a.k.a. Gen Z) hasn't known a world without technology at all. So, of course, this generation will not relate to those of us who use technology as a tool, not as our primary means of connection. We need to build bridges between how we all give and receive information, and that's where our work begins.

PRACTICES FOR SUCCESS

Building Bridges

The communication work I do helps people more effectively give and receive information regardless of generation, position, age, gender, or anything else. It's so effective we call the program "Results Guaranteed" because we teach people how to recognize the ways in which we can work to meet anyone's priorities and needs if we're willing to understand them. This means investing the time to learn about others and their motivations. Do they need more information? Do they find meaning in their relationships at work and in the work they do? Do they need others to cut the chatter and get to the point? Are they excited by the work they're doing and the people they work with? We have to begin there, or the statistics and labeling will limit what's possible between us.

Millennials get a bad rap, yet are they really that different from any other generation of people? When we researched the common millennial traits we hear about most often, we realized millennials share at least five attributes with entrepreneurs:

1. They desire to change the world.
2. They want to design life on their own terms.
3. They value relationships.
4. They don't accept the status quo.
5. They have an insatiable hunger to learn.

The research and our conversations about generations tend to focus on the differences. Therefore, the differences are what we see. If, instead, we begin from the common ground we share, while still recognizing the differences, we can build bridges and begin to gracefully work through the tough stuff. To learn more about the program or to see our blog, use the link at the end of this chapter.

MAXIMIZE SUCCESS

Beth Kieffer Leonard and Kimpa Moss

Managing Partner Beth Kieffer Leonard and COO Kimpa Moss have led the accounting firm Lurie LLP through both internal and external change, resulting in numerous best-place-to-work awards and significant growth in the firm. This dynamic duo leads with their values and invites employees to participate in the future of Lurie LLP.

One of their biggest initiatives is an Emerging Leaders program. As Beth explains:

I had a dream of running a firm that reflected the values I thought were important. I wanted to treat our partners equally; I wanted to have a line of clients out the door and a line out the door for talent. If we wanted to be a destination for talent during the tightest talent race for accountants ever, how would we become a place where people want to work this hard and feel it's worth it? You only win if you win the talent war.

I knew we needed to keep these high-potential candidates or we'd lose them to another business. So, I brought a futurist in, the brilliant Watts Wacker. We told him about our program and he said, "If you want to live this and you want to make a difference, you need to invite them in to your annual meeting." We were all skeptical, but I thought the worst that could happen was we'd just never do it again. So we did it and it totally changed everything. There were twelve people in that group, two from each department, both men and women, and they participated in dreaming about what the firm of the future looked like. Then they became a cohort and led part of the all-firm annual meeting, to be seen as leaders and take on projects. They were engaged and knew we were investing in them. And they received partner time.

Kimpa has found employees are eager to share the ideas they have, and Beth says this is part of building consensus:

"People feel like they're part of the change instead of having change thrown at them. People feel like they're heard."

LEARNING TOGETHER

For my daughter, Alexandra, and me, mentorship isn't a sit-down-and-I'll-teach-you situation; it's a series of daily interactions. This daily communication is important to keep Alexandra on track, show her I'm consistently invested in her learning, and provide the opportunity for the open conversations we need to understand each other. What often surprises me is that the insights I think might be impactful or important are not, typically, the ones Alexandra takes to heart from our interactions; the observations I'd consider commonplace oftentimes seem to Alexandra to be the most interesting. As Alexandra herself explains:

> One example is how I learned to speak intelligently about what we do in our business. When I first began working with Sue, I didn't know how to do that. There was no script to memorize, and I never really sat down with Sue and practiced it or wrote down talking points. Because Sue invites me to events with her, I'm able to sit in the back of the room and experience her doing keynotes and talking about our business. I've learned to pitch through observation and practice. Listening to Sue working with leaders and presenting at events taught me how to speak intelligently about our services.

> Another thing I learned was how to dress professionally because there's no class in college to teach you how to look as a professional person. But it's a really important thing

because it helps our clients feel comfortable and respected. Once, I came to work in something that was a bit over the line: a short dress that had an open back. Sue said it was cute for a date but not for work, and she sent me home to change. Honestly, I was upset; I felt like my personal brand was being challenged. Sue helped me understand that our clients come before that, and dressing professionally shows them respect. That made complete sense to me and I've been open to feedback on my attire since then. A useful piece of advice Sue shared was, "If you're questioning whether you should wear something, the answer is no." I still use this advice and share it frequently.

PRACTICES FOR SUCCESS

Daily Check-Ins

Don't assume people you're mentoring haven't asked a question because they already know the answer. Be proactive with your mentees, and make daily check-ins or huddles a habit for you both. It gives them a chance to air their thoughts and ask questions. You'll be able to more quickly identify where the gaps are and prioritize all that's happening with your mentees, and they'll learn how to solve future problems or concerns based on your responses to current questions. If your mentees are not a part of your organization, communicate more frequently with them than you think you need to. A quick e-mail or text will go a long way. Younger people new in their career need interaction. Make time for them frequently. It shows you care.

As I explained to Alexandra, you need to dress for the position you want, not the one you have. In other words, suit up for the sport you're playing. If you are playing football, you wear a certain uniform. If you're playing basketball, you wear a different uniform, and if you try to play football wearing a basketball uniform, you're going to get killed. The game we're playing happens to be business, and it's got its own uniform. You have to dress as well as, or better than, your clients do or it's game over. This made sense to her once I shared the larger *why*, and she appreciated the fact that I had taken the time to have that conversation.

TEACHING FOLLOW-THROUGH

As a company, we set ninety-day priorities we call Rocks, which are part of the Entrepreneurial Operating System™ (EOS®, see chapter 9). When you set them, you're saying, "These are the priorities I commit to accomplishing by the end of the quarter." Rocks aren't part of your everyday job; they're above and beyond it. Alexandra ambitiously set five Rocks one particular quarter, which is a lot, but she was confident she would accomplish them.

When it comes to goal setting, I'm either your worst nightmare or your best teammate, because I'm the person who ensures that if you say you're going to do something, you will get it done. I will help you, *and* I will push you. We were about eight weeks into a thirteen-week quarter, and Ali put her Rocks on our issues list, and we began to discuss them. She asked whether I could help her prioritize her Rocks.

I said, "No. You're asking which one you can skip or delay or put off or not do, but they're all prioritized, they're all number one. You'll need to get them *all* done. How you'll get them done, I don't know. You have five weeks remaining. So how can we help you; what do you need from us?"

That message wasn't received well initially, but by the end of the meeting, Alexandra was saying things such as, "I guess I'm going to have to grow up and work some nights and probably some weekends. I'll ask for help as I need it and I'm going to get these done."

That meeting and the weeks following were a turning point for Alexandra. She went from "I'm going to have this nice little life where I will work forty hours a week and hang out with my friends and go to brunch," to "If I want to be in this business, it's going to require more of me." It was one of those moments when I witnessed her becoming a different, more extraordinary human being. And she was victorious when she completed those Rocks. We celebrated. It is an incredible responsibility as well as an amazing gift to help someone grow profoundly. Her success inspires me every day, and I'm grateful she was willing to hear my advice. I was able to hold the line and have a tough conversation while coming from a place of care. I communicated my intentions, and Alexandra was able to receive my feedback and coaching.

"It really was a big personal shift," Alexandra says, "something that will serve me my entire life, whether professionally or personally. When I think about mentoring and how Sue has worked with me, it's really gotten deeper for me. I'm still learning, and it's hard work. But to have someone on your team who really cares about you and is patient with you and wants to support you is just invaluable."

When Alexandra joined the team, part of her learning was about showing up for work, how to behave in a meeting, and how to facilitate one. Regardless of her college degree and good grades, there was a lot Alexandra had to learn in order to thrive in the fast-paced world of small business.

"When I was in high school and thinking about getting a job," Alexandra says, "my dad told me not to because my job was to get good grades and into a prestigious college. What's interesting, looking back, is how little of my learning in college is applicable to my job. I enjoyed what I studied and use my writing skills daily, but almost everything I do at YESS! I've had to learn on the job. It feels as if I've gone to college twice, and I think that emphasizes how little of what you study in college matters. I had the false assumption that when I received my college degree I would have learned everything I needed in order to be successful in a career. Now I've learned that isn't the case, and even Sue is constantly learning new things. When we go to meetings and conferences, we debrief afterward and discuss what we learned from them.

"I've also had to learn how to implement knowledge once I've studied it. My college career was strictly liberal arts oriented: read a book, write a paper, take a test. There was never any practice of applying the knowledge in a real way to prove you've learned it; you just took the test. In the working world, you always must apply what you've learned; this step is a skill I'm still working on."

PRACTICES FOR SUCCESS

Share a Big Enough Why

Alexandra and I were attending a millennial workshop where the millennials were separated from the other attendees and asked a series of questions, such as, "Why do you have to dress in a certain way for meetings?" To the millennials, these seemed like a lot of dumb, arbitrary rules. The nonmillennials in the other room believed employees should dress to show

> respect for their audience and themselves. Once that was explained to the millennials, once they understood the *why*, they were fine with it. As my mentor rubye Erickson taught, "When you give someone a big enough *why*, they'll handle the *what* and the *how*."

Speaking of a big enough *why*, Alexandra and I stumbled into one when she joined me at the WPO annual conference. Until I came into her life, Alexandra had never met a woman who worked in business. Suddenly, at the conference, we were surrounded by over eight hundred women business owners. Alexandra was inspired, and I was moved to tears when she shared how seeing all those women leaders made her believe, for the first time, she too could be a CEO. We wondered if there weren't other young women like Alexandra who were unaware of the opportunities small business offered. Out of that insight, we created the Women's Entrepreneurial Experience (WEE). The program paired women ages eighteen through thirty with female business owners from the WPO, and we had over eighty women at some of our events. The young women learned from the seasoned business owners and, in turn, the business owners enjoyed sharing their wisdom and having to think differently because of the questions the younger generations asked. It was a valuable experience for all who participated, and they were united around the bigger *why:* why we celebrate the 2 percent of multimillion-dollar, women-owned businesses in the USA.

That's the essence of it: seizing an opportunity and learning together. It doesn't have to be your daughter, although I nearly burst with pride when I hear accolades about how Alexandra conducts herself. When we were at the annual WPO conference together, one of my friends told me, "I'm so inspired by you and Alexandra. In ten years, when she's old enough, I want my daughter to join me at the conference. If I can have one night like this with my daughter, it would be worth it. To see what you two are doing and how you're participating like this gives me hope for us all."

BE WILLING TO OVERCOMMUNICATE

Young people new to their careers need more communication, not less. They've grown up with a wealth of global information available at any moment through their devices. They need to be met with, and talked with, and the relationship needs to be nurtured on a regular basis. I work far more independently than any of the young people I know. Most of them are used to working in teams and collaborating. When I'm not touching bases and either listening or checking in, it can go south pretty fast.

"Because my generation received rewards and recognition for everything," Alexandra says, "I assume I've done a bad job if I don't receive positive feedback. In reality, it's the opposite: if I did a bad job or anyone on our team was unhappy with my work, they'd address it with me directly. Realizing I had this need took some work and reframing. Now I'll coach myself: 'Okay, no news is good news; don't jump off the deep end because you didn't hear anything.'"

Alexandra's orientation is very different from the way I was brought up: I was informed I wouldn't be told I'd done a great job unless I'd done an exceedingly great job. Otherwise, I should assume everything was fine. I don't believe it has to do with a sense of entitlement. I believe this generation's need for affirmation is a product of how young people today were raised. They need more frequent affirmation to assess their performance. Minus that affirmation, they'll assume the worst. When both parties are willing to reframe, it's easy to build a bridge. As a mentor, you have to demonstrate you care, be consistent, and be firm. You hold the line. You wake people up when they're asleep to the impact of their behavior. You say things that are meant to shatter some of their illusions. Interestingly, during the process, your mentee winds up teaching you a *lot* because it's never a one-way relationship. If you're not learning as much as your mentee, something's not working.

The key is we're both vested. Speaking as a mentor and mentee, it's a tremendously rewarding relationship. I believe you're not a leader until you produce a leader who produces a leader. Until that happens two generations beyond you, it's not leadership, because most people can influence those in their immediate proximity. The true test is whether you can have an impact that goes beyond one generation to inspire and inform the next generation. As a leader, I need to be as receptive and open as I expect the people I'm leading to be. If I'm operating merely from the perspective of a teacher who believes there's nothing to learn from the students, there's a power disparity, and that won't work in our world.

PRACTICES FOR SUCCESS

Set Clear Expectations

No matter what generation you're from, make sure your mentee, employee, or teammate understands exactly what you want, how you want it, and the specific timeline they need to adhere to. If you weren't explicitly clear, you can't blame people for not meeting your expectations. After all, they come from a different generation than you do and may not have the same ideas about what is relevant, necessary, and appropriate in business. This is why communication is so important. As Alexandra explains:

> Sue has taught me that over-communicating is important between teammates as well, not just mentors to mentees. Someone may be from the same genera-tion as you or in the same position in the company, but that does not mean their communication style matches yours. I recently encountered this when we hired a new employee, who's just a bit younger than I am. We clicked immediately and I couldn't wait to become friends as well as teammates. Things started off well, but after a few months, there was tension between us. She often relied on me for training and help, and while I was happy to give it, I was also struggling with my own workload. I'd often ask if her requests for help could wait until the end of the day or the following day, and when she did not push back, I assumed that timeline worked for us both.
>
> This tension was there and I noticed it, but little did I know it had to do with me. I simply assumed she didn't like the position. After all, if she had a problem with me, wouldn't she speak with me directly? This was a poor assump-tion on my end. Eventually she aired her frustrations to another teammate about me. They came to me and suggested I speak to her directly. I was a bit surprised and defensive at first. Then Sue coached me about how to have what I imagined would be a difficult conversation.
>
> Monday morning I told her I needed to speak with her and set the stage by assuring her that regardless of

work, I valued our friendship and liked her as a person. This was important. I shared what I'd heard and asked her to give me the feedback directly. I listened as she openly shared her frustrations. This was good learning for me, and I asked for examples so I could better understand. When she had finished, I shared my side, explaining why I had reacted as I did, realizing I had only had partial information from her. I emphasized to her my reactions were never personal; they were involuntary.

Ultimately, we were able to meet in the middle. She committed to communicating directly and more frequently. I committed to working more effectively with her. Sue sat in on the conversation, which neutralized our emotions. When it was complete, Sue suggested we have lunch together that day and spend time together as friends. This was immensely helpful and we spent a half hour laughing, catching up, and moving beyond our original conversation. It went so well we've committed to doing it every week. Our work relationship is better than it's ever been, and we are both happier and more effective due to that conversation.

MYTHS ABOUT MILLENNIALS

Millennials sometimes get a bad rap in the working world, and there are a few particularly damaging myths that have attached themselves to this generation that I'd like to take a moment to dispel.

First is the biggie: they suffer from an inflated sense of entitlement. In some regards, with some people, it is probably true, although it seems unfair to label an entire generation. In my experience of working with millennials, I honestly don't see much of it. I believe they are really quite open, and the onus is on us to reach out and make time to connect with them. As leaders, we need to take the time to communicate, create meaning, and listen. Yes, they need direction—business parenting, even—to help them present themselves professionally in the working world. But what generation hasn't come into the workplace with a lot to learn?

Some people are put off by their need to know the *why* for the things they're asked to do. When I observe them, this need seems to spring from how sincerely they want to make a difference; they want their work to have meaning. I find I don't get pushback in the way others seem to in their workplaces. When I sit down with Alexandra, I do so with care and with the clear intent of helping her to be better. I make it clear how her role and actions contribute to our business and affect others, including our clients, during both positive and negative outcomes.

Yes, millennials use their electronic devices a lot, but if they're using them to further the business or themselves, that's great. Good people have a moral compass, so I don't monitor time; I monitor outcomes. Of course, if they're not getting their work done, or they're negatively impacting their team, it's a different discussion. If things are being accomplished, I think connecting and communicating is the right way to impact this generation.

"Being engaged with work, clients, and teammates," Alexandra says, "is important to us. And that's something Sue fosters in our company: We're very relational with our clients, which I appreciate, so if I have to stay late, I don't mind. I don't resent it because I know I'm helping a person I care about. As long as I have a meaningful reason, I'm good."

Entrepreneurs and millennials have many shared values; while the way they express those values might look a bit different, the root is the same. When we use communication to clearly identify shared values, everyone is motivated and on the same page. Frequent, clear communication is the key to working effectively with people of different backgrounds. You must work to uncover the common ground and lead with that. If people know you sincerely care and are on their team, they will do what it takes to work well with you.

Believing generational (or any other) stereotypes limits your ability to harness the best from everyone at the table. Engaging everyone around shared values and remembering to be graceful as you communicate through the tough stuff will go a long way to bridging the generational divide. We have more to gain working together than we do focusing on our differences.

How can we move from seeing the barriers between us to a place of common ground and opportunity? It begins with conversations, courageous, open-minded, open-ended conversations expanding on what each participant brings and maximizing it in concert with the others present. This is how we begin to gracefully work through the tough stuff and drop our preconceived notions about what's possible with others. We will become unstoppable when we take the time to truly connect with each other, finding the common ground to begin the conversations.

For bonus information, practices, and resources:
www.ChasingPerfection.net/book/chapter-10

CONCLUSION

The reality remains that being a leader requires taking risks, creating opportunities out of problems, and venturing out onto the skinny branches. That's where you, as a leader, are at your best, and it isn't easy. Venturing onto those branches is accompanied by your humanity, which includes vulnerability. As Patrick Lencioni says, "Success is not a matter of mastering subtle, sophisticated theory, but rather of embracing common sense with uncommon levels of discipline and persistence."

In order to maximize success, you must have practices to shatter the illusions you have and stop chasing perfection. The practices contained in this book are common sense, requiring discipline and persistence to sustain yourself as a leader. They're required, not optional. By mastering them, you will reach a place where you're truly at peace and in touch with yourself, and nothing anyone says or does bothers you, and no negativity or drama can touch you. It means being at the pinnacle of whatever you do; you are the ultimate leader you can be. We say, **this IS it;** you're at the top of your game, the desired space to be; you're unf♥<kwithable.

To see where you are on the unf♥<kwithability scale,
visit our website at:
www.ChasingPerfection.net/book/unfscale

LEADERS IN THIS BOOK

1. Beth Bronfman: founder and managing partner of View, The Agency: www.viewtheagency.com

2. Nancy Lyons: founder and CEO of Clockwork, speaker: www.clockwork.com, www.nancylyons.com

3. ReBecca (Becky) Koenig Roloff: president of St. Catherine University: www.stkate.edu

4. Susan Denk: owner of White Crane Construction: www.whitecraneconstruction.com

5. Anita Janssen, serial entrepreneur: https://www.linkedin.com/in/anita-janssen-a48735124/

6. Rhoda Olsen, CEO of Great Clips, Inc.: www.greatclips.com

7. Amy Ronneberg, president of Be the Match: www.bethematch.org

8. Roz Alford, cofounder of ASAP Solutions Group; managing director of Women Impacting Public Policy (WIPP): www.wipp.org

9. Sandy Hansen-Wolff, CEO of AgVenture Feed & Seed: www.agventurefeeds.com

10. Laurie Wondra, owner and shaman of YourLifeCore, and IT executive : www.yourlifecore.com

11. Marsha Firestone, PhD, founder and president of the Women Presidents' Organization: www.womenpresidentsorg.com

12. Mahtab Rezai, principal and CEO of Crux Collaborative: www.cruxcollaborative.com

13. Julie Allinson, founder of eyebobs: www.eyebobs.com

14. Kate Grathwol, president/CEO of Vision Loss Resources and Contract Production Services: www.visionlossresources.org, www.cpsworkshop.com

15. Amelia Mata, owner and CEO of Hennepin Home Health Care, and Under the Weather: www.hennhomecare.com, www.utwsickcare.com

16. Kay Phillips, cofounder and former president of ATEK Companies: www.atekcompanies.com

17. Lisa David, partner at eCapital Advisors: www.ecapitaladvisors.com

18. Beth Kieffer Leonard, managing partner of Lurie LLP: www.luriellp.com

19. Kimpa Moss, COO of Lurie LLP: www.luriellp.com

WAYS TO REACH US

EMAIL:
sue@sayyess.com (general: info@sayyess.com)

WEBSITE:
www.sayyess.com

www.suehawkes.com

www.ChasingPerfection.net

BLOG:
www.ChasingPerfection.net/blog

FACEBOOK:
www.facebook.com/ChasingPerfectionBook/

TWITTER:
@SueHawkesYESS

LINKEDIN:
https://www.linkedin.com/in/suehawkes/

INSTAGRAM:
@suehawkes

OFFICE PHONE:
612-718-1699

REFERENCES

CHAPTER ONE

UNMASKING YOUR SUPERHERO

Clance, Pauline Rose and Suzanne Ament Imes. 1978. "The Imposter Phenomenon in High Achieving Women: Dynamics and Therapeutic Intervention." *Psychotherapy: Theory, Research & Practice* 15, no. 3: 241–47, doi:10.1037/h0086006.

Langford, Joe and Pauline Rose Clance. 1993. "The Imposter Phenomenon: Recent Research Findings Regarding Dynamics, Personality and Family Patterns and Their Implications for Treatment." *Psychotherapy: Theory, Research, Practice, Training* 30, no. 3: 495–501, doi:10.1037/0033-3204.30.3.495.

Sakulku, J. "The Impostor Phenomenon." 2011. *International Journal of Behavioral Science* 6, no. 1: 73–92.

Archor, S. 2017. "The Happiness Advantage." Speech presented at the Women Presidents' Organization International Meeting in Orlando, Florida, May 4.

CHAPTER TWO

BALANCE IS BULLSHIT

Wickman, G. and R. Boer. 2016. *How to Be a Great Boss*. Dallas, TX: BenBella Books.

CHAPTER FIVE

INTUITION IS YOUR SUPERPOWER

The Oxford dictionary. Oxford: Oxford University Press, 1992.

Isaacson, W. 2011. "The Genius of Jobs." Accessed July 24, 2017, http://www.nytimes.com/2011/10/30/opinion/sunday/steve-jobs-genius.html.

Wilderness Survival. Quiz, Interpretive Service, Monroe County (New York) Parks Department.

Gladwell, M. 2013. *Blink: The Power of Thinking without Thinking*. New York: Back Bay Books.

Kornfield, Jack. *A path with heart: a guide through the perils and promises of spiritual life*. New York, NY: Bantam Books, 1993.

CHAPTER SIX

GAME CHANGERS AND TRAILBLAZERS

Watson, Emma. 2014. Speech by UN Women Goodwill Ambassador Emma Watson at the HeForShe campaign, United Nations Headquarters, New York, September 20. Television broadcast. http://webtv.un.org/search/launch-of-the-heforshe-campaign-special-event/3797140848001/?term=heforshe.

CHAPTER SEVEN

BACKWARD AND IN HEELS

Feloni, R. 2015. Tony Robbins describes his intense morning routine. Business Insider. Accessed July 24, 2017, http://www.businessinsider. com/tony-robbins-morning-routine-2015-10.

Rose, M. 2015. "What Does Michael Phelps Do before a Race?" *The Guardian*, January 29, 1992. Accessed July 23, 2017, http://www. livestrong.com/article/1002130-michael-phelps-before-race.

Mehta, Pavithra K. 2014. "The World's Greatest Business Case for Compassion." Speech to Women Presidents' Organization 2014 International Meeting, New Orleans, June 24.

CHAPTER EIGHT

POURING GAS ON THE FIRE

"You must be the change you want to see in the world" Unknown source, often incorrectly attributed to Mahatma Ghandhi (paraphrased).

Morton, B. 2011. "Falser Words Were Never Spoken." Accessed July 24, 2017, http://www.nytimes.com/2011/08/30/opinion/falser-words-were-never-spoken.html.

Ranseth, J. 2017. Gandhi didn't actually say, "Be the change you want to see in the world." Here's the real quote. Accessed July 24, 2017, https://josephranseth.com/gandhi-didnt-say-be-the-change-you-want-to-see-in-the-world/.

CHAPTER NINE

UNLEARNING TO LEARN

Gardner, H. 2011. *Frames of Mind: The Theory of Multiple Intelligences*. New York: Basic Books.

Gardner, H. 2003. *Multiple Intelligences: The Theory in Practice*. New York: Basic Books.

Armstrong, T. 1999. *7 Kinds of Smart: Identifying and Developing Your Multiple Intelligences*. New York: Plume.

Wickman, G. 2011. *Traction: Get a Grip on Your Business*. Dallas, TX: BenBella Books

CHAPTER TEN

ENTITLED TO ENLIGHTENED

Wickman, G. *Traction: Get a Grip on Your Business*. Dallas, TX: BenBella Books.

Harnish, V. 2011. *Mastering the Rockefeller Habits: What You Must Do to Increase the Value of Your Growing Firm*. Ashburn, VA: Gazelles Publishing.

Covey, Stephen, A. Roger Merrill, and Rebecca R. Merrill. 2017. *First Things First*. New York: Simon & Schuster.

CONCLUSION

Lencioni, Patrick. 2002. *The Five Dysfunctions of a Team: A Leadership Fable*. San Francisco: Jossey-Bass.

Lencioni, Patrick. 2005. *Overcoming the Five Dysfunctions of a Team: A Field Guide for Leaders, Managers, and Facilitators*. San Francisco: Jossey-Bass.